FAST & EASY TECHNIQUES FOR
BUILDING MODERN
Cabinetry
Danny Proulx

READ THIS IMPORTANT SAFETY NOTICE

To prevent accidents, keep safety in mind while you work. Use the safety guards installed on power equipment; they are for your protection. When working on power equipment, keep fingers away from saw blades, wear safety goggles to prevent injuries from flying wood chips and sawdust, wear headphones to protect your hearing, and consider installing a dust vacuum to reduce the amount of airborne sawdust in your woodshop. Don't wear loose clothing, such as neckties or shirts with loose sleeves, or jewelry, such as rings, necklaces or bracelets, when working on power equipment. Tie back long hair to prevent it from getting caught in your equipment. People who are sensitive to certain chemicals should check the chemical content of any product before using it. The author and editors who compiled this book have tried to make the contents as accurate and correct as possible. Plans, illustrations, photographs and text have been carefully checked. All instructions, plans and projects should be carefully read, studied and understood before beginning construction. Due to the variability of local conditions, construction materials, skill levels, etc., neither the author nor Popular Woodworking Books assumes any responsibility for any accidents, injuries, damages or other losses incurred resulting from the material presented in this book.

METRIC CONVERSION CHART

TO CONVERT	TO	MULTIPLY BY
Inches	Centimeters	2.54
Centimeters	Inches	0.4
Feet	Centimeters	30.5
Centimeters	Feet	0.03
Yards	Meters	0.9
Meters	Yards	1.1
Sq. Inches	Sq. Centimeters	6.45
Sq. Centimeters	Sq. Inches	0.16
Sq. Feet	Sq. Meters	0.09
Sq. Meters	Sq. Feet	10.8
Sq. Yards	Sq. Meters	0.8
Sq. Meters	Sq. Yards	1.2
Pounds	Kilograms	0.45
Kilograms	Pounds	2.2
Ounces	Grams	28.4
Grams	Ounces	0.04

A DAVID & CHARLES BOOK

First published in the UK in 2001
First published in the USA in 2000 by Popular Woodworking Books,
an imprint of F&W Publications, Inc., 1507 Dana Avenue, Cincinnati, Ohio, 45027

Copyright © Danny Proulx

Danny Proulx has asserted his right to be identified as author of this work in accordance with the Copyright, Designs and Patents Act, 1988.

A catalogue record for this book is available from the British Library.

ISBN 0 7153 1215 4

Manufactured in China for David & Charles
Brunel House Newton Abbot Devon

Conceived, designed and produced by Popular Woodworking Books, an imprint of F&W Publications, Inc.

Edited by Michael Berger
Cover designed by Brian Roeth
Production coordinated by Emily Gross
Step-by-Step Photography by Danny Proulx
Cover and Chapter Lead Photography by Michael Bowie, Lux Photography, 95 Beech St.,
    Ottawa, Ont., (613)-563-7199
Computer Illustrations by Len Churchill, Lenmark Communications Ltd., 590 Alden Rd.,
    Suite 206, Markham, Ont., (905)-475-5222
Workshop Site provided by Rideau Cabinets, P.O. Box 331, Russell, Ont., K4R 1E1,
    (613)-445-3722

Dedication

Writing any type of project book requires a lot of help. Without those special people the tasks would be much harder if not impossible.

This book is dedicated to my wife Gale, my woodworking assistant Jack Chaters, and our photographic wizard Michael Bowie.

A new "team" member, Len Churchill, created the great graphic illustrations. Many thanks for his wonderful work.

And I also want to thank the staff at Popular Woodworking Books. They are always ready to help and do make writing these books a pleasure.

The great layout work is the creation of two fine editors; Mark Thompson and Michael Berger. They make life easy!

About the Author

Danny Proulx has been involved in the woodworking field for more than 30 years. He has operated a custom kitchen cabinet shop since 1989.

He is a contributing editor to *CabinetMaker* magazine and has published articles in other magazines such as *Canadian Home Workshop*, *Popular Woodworking*, *WoodShop News*, and *Homes & Cottages*.

His earlier books include *Build Your Own Kitchen Cabinets*, *The Kitchen Cabinetmaker's Building and Business Manual*, *How to Build Classic Garden Furniture* and *Smart Shelving and Storage Solutions*.

His web site address is www.cabinetmaking.com and he can be reached by email at danny@cabinetmaking.com.

Acknowledgments

Many suppliers have contributed products, material and technical support during the project building phase.

I appreciate how helpful they've been and recommend the companies without hesitation.

Julius Blum, Inc.
(800) 438-6788
www.blum.com

Delta International Machinery Corp.
(800) 438-2486
www.deltawoodworking.com

L.R.H Enterprises, Inc.
(800) 423-2544
www.lrhent.com

Rout-R-Slide
Jessem Tool Co.
(800) 436-6799
www.jessem.com

Ryobi Canada, Inc.
(800) 265-6778
www.ryobi.com

Tenryu America, Inc.
(800) 951-7297
www.tenryu.com

Wolfcraft, Inc.
(630) 773-4777
www.wolfcraft.com

Table of Contents

Introduction

Woodworking is a hobby for some and a profession for a few of us. I'm lucky enough to be able to write and have fun building projects. It is an enjoyable experience. But I have one goal with my writing and that is to teach new techniques with each book.

Anyone can follow a step-by-step plan and complete the project. However, if you haven't learned anything in the process, all you're left with is a project.

There are many useful projects in this book. And I've tried to show new techniques and materials with each one. That's the reason I offer construction options. Hopefully, you can apply the building lessons to other projects or modify the ones in this book to better suit your needs.

The first chapter deals with many of the new hardware items that have been introduced over the last few years. Quite a number of them have been adopted as standard items in the cabinet-making trade. They make project building a lot more fun and much more interesting.

Throughout the book I've tried to build each project without any fancy tools. You shouldn't have to invest a fortune to enjoy woodworking. So, each project has been designed with that concept in mind. When there is a need for more advanced tools I've tried to offer alternatives. You can build all the furniture with a circular saw and a few other inexpensive electric tools. I've done it, and I believe the majority of people can also successfully build them.

There are three work center plans: One for adults, one for teenagers, and a great closet-conversion study center for the younger children.

Entertainment units are popular, and I've designed a project that should interest even the most demanding person. You can modify it to suit your tastes by altering a couple of dimensions.

Two chapters cover basic cabinetmaking. The base and upper units offered here can be used in the kitchen, laundry room, basement or workshop. These cabinets have literally hundreds of uses, and a chart is provided for all of the standard widths. If you want a nonstandard width, I've detailed the process for building and explained how to calculate door sizes.

Display cases are always popular items. The techniques for building the case here, as well as customizing your own, are explained.

Pantry cabinets and wardrobes solve many storage problems around the home. Both of these projects are fully detailed and both are easy to build.

Dressers, chests and beds are fun to build and, with the new hardware available today, simple to put together. The platform bed offered here would make some youngster happy. You can construct it in one weekend!

Have fun building and learn some new techniques. I've enjoyed building each one, and I'm sure you will, too. Let me know how your project has turned out by dropping me an E-mail at danny@cabinetmaking.com

CHAPTER I

Modern Materials and Hardware

The last few years have been exciting for those of us in the building materials and hardware business. Modern plywood, improved particleboard (PB), melamine-coated particleboard (MPB) and medium density fiberboard (MDF) have made a tremendous impact on how we build cabinets.

We've come to realize that our forest products must be managed carefully. Wood that was once burned or discarded as garbage has now become a valuable resource. Improved management of that wood has been a blessing to all of us who care about our forests.

That so-called garbage wood is now used to manufacture all forms of particle core and fiberboards. It has become popular as a cabinet-making material in the commercial casework industry and is now being accepted by the hobbyist woodworker.

Some of us used these composite boards when they were first introduced and may have been disappointed. Today, there are grades and standards, and the products are far superior to the early offerings.

Although low cost sheet material is available, it isn't good value for your money and should be avoided. Ask the supplier for cabinet-grade products and pay a little more to get high-quality material. Most often, it's only a few dollars a sheet more, but it's well worth the money. You can make a lot of furniture from one sheet of MPB, so a few extra dollars isn't a major issue.

These modern sheet goods and hardware have opened a whole new world. You don't have to be an expert cabinetmaker to build great-looking projects. And you don't need a fully equipped shop. You can build most of these projects with only a few inexpensive tools.

Joinery Techniques

The butt joint, using modern hardware, is the most common joinery method. Most adhesives are not suited to properly join many of the coated materials with the exception of wood veneer material. Melamine, which is a paper soaked in resins and fused to PB, cannot be glued with standard wood adhesives. We therefore depend on high-quality fasteners to build our cabinets.

CAPPED DECORATIVE SCREWS Other decorative screws for PB have screw-on caps that are available in many finishes. These caps can be matched to complement the coated PB's surface. And when properly located on the project they look great.

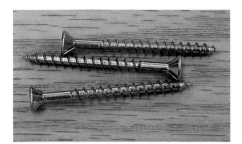

PARTICLEBOARD SCREWS PB or chipboard screws are available from most hardware suppliers. They have a thin shaft with a coarse thread and are specially designed to hold PB securely.

DECORATIVE CHIPBOARD SCREWS Variations of these screws include ones with decorative heads. These are meant to be seen and add a finished look to the cabinet.

SCREW-HOLE COVER CAPS When working with wood-veneer-covered PBs, we have dozens of wood screw-hole coverings available. The plug and button are the two common types but many other styles are available.

PLASTIC SCREW CAPS There are plastic caps held on by the screw, and push-on styles that fit in the screw head.

COMMERCIAL PB FASTENERS A special PB screw is available that, until recently, has been used only by professional cabinetmakers. It's a great fastener, with superior holding capabilities, but you should be aware of a couple of issues when using this screw.

First, the screw is tapered and requires a special, and somewhat expensive, drill bit. Secondly, this fastener has a large-diameter body and coarse thread. You must drill an accurate pilot hole and drive the screw straight into that hole for a positive hold. Poor drilling techniques or improper driving will push the screw through the finished surface or weaken the joint.

However, once you become accustomed to using the screw you'll appreciate its fastening power. When you need a strong joint that is able to withstand stress, this is the fastener to use.

DECORATIVE BOLTS Furniture that can be taken apart is a necessary requirement for some people. That need has led to the development of a whole range of joinery bolts. Furniture can be quickly taken apart and rebuilt without damage.

Cabinet and furniture makers have developed many applications for this type of fastener. It's often seen on children's beds and storage shelving systems. The Europeans have expanded the use of these bolts and developed an extensive line of knock down furniture.

Hidden Joinery Hardware

Many types of quick-connect-and-release right angle butt joinery hardware items are available. Often, a screwdriver is all that is needed to assemble the furniture. And it can be taken apart quickly if the need arises.

I'll use some of these hardware items to build a few of the projects in this book. It may not be purist woodworking, but these fasteners do have a place in modern cabinetry.

FINISHED END CAPS Another version of bolt joinery uses a finished end cap. The bolt is often hidden and only the cap is visible. The head is about ½" in diameter and is drawn tight to the material surface.

METAL END CAPS These cap nuts provide a sound mechanical connection. They are also used on high-stress joints such as bed frames.

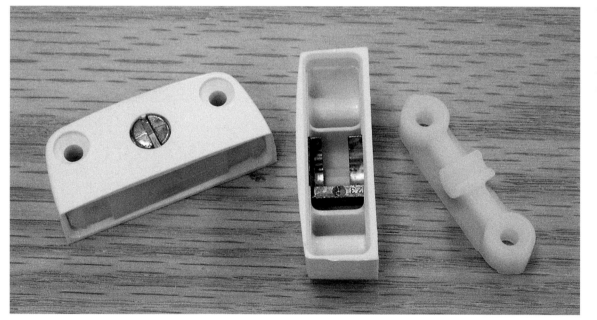

QUICK CONNECT HIDDEN HARDWARE Quick-connect hardware is common in some furniture designs.

CAM LOCKS Most quick-connect hardware operates on a cam lock system, as shown here.

HIDDEN AND TRADITIONAL HINGES

To some degree, the modern European or hidden hinge has replaced the traditional-style hinge. But there continues to be a need for our old standby model. In certain applications, it is the hinge of choice.

In the last few years door-mounting hardware from Europe has become a very popular alternative. The so-called Euro hidden hinge is now widely used as the standard kitchen cabinet door hardware.

The hidden hinge usually requires a 35mm hole drilled in the door. That task seems a bit challenging to some people but it's a straightforward process.

There is a learning curve when working with the hidden hinge. For instance, these hinges are classified with terms such as full overlay, half overlay, and inset. The distance the door covers the cabinet side member (gable end) is called overlay.

Parts of a Hinge

The hidden hinge comes in two parts: The hinge, or boss, which is mounted on the door, and the mounting plate, which is attached to the cabinet side or gable end of the cabinet.

The boss is attached to the mounting plate with a screw or a clip pin. The clip-on method is becoming popular because you can remove the door from the mounting plate without disturbing any adjustments.

Degrees of Operation

Hidden hinges are also classed in terms of degrees of opening. For standard door applications, the 100° to 110° opening hinge is common. But you can purchase hinges that will allow the door to open from 90° to 170°. The term simply refers to the number of degrees of swing that the door can open from its closed position.

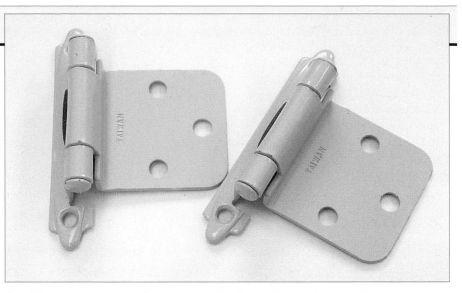

The old standby traditional style hinge can still be for used for overlay doors. It is easily mounted to the door and then onto the cabinet face. It provides a 180° swing.

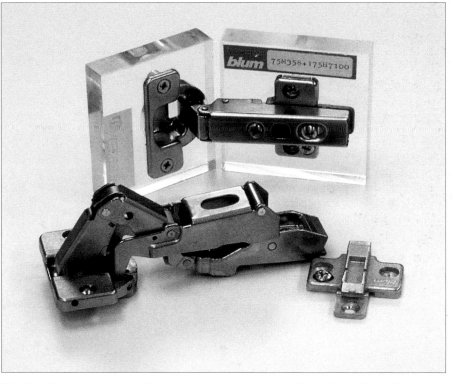

The Euro hinge and mounting plate system is used on many modern cabinets. It provides great flexiblity in door mounting options.

Adjustable Shelving

The fixed shelf is gone! Nowadays, everyone wants adjustable shelves in their cabinets. This feature makes sense because it increases the flexibility of any cabinet.

Adjustable shelving is easy to install. All that is required are accurately drilled columns of holes and good-quality shelf pins. Quite a few of the projects in this book will feature adjustable shelving.

Assembly Brackets

Attaching countertops during a kitchen project is often accomplished using metal brackets. It's the best method for securing something, like a kitchen countertop, which will have to be replaced in the future.

These brackets come in many shapes and sizes. They provide a quick-connect capability and add strength to any project. They are sometimes used with other joinery hardware to provide extra hold when joint stress is an issue.

Drawer Glides

Modern hardware now gives us the opportunity to vary drawer styles and construction methods. Side and bottom mounted glides with three-quarter and full extension capabilities, along with positive stops and closing features have opened a world of design opportunities.

Low-cost metal drawer glide sets that consist of two bottom-mounted drawer runners and two cabinet tracks are simple to install. Installing the new drawer hardware demands special attention to the drawer body width, as most of the hardware requires precise clearances to operate properly. Otherwise, building high-quality drawers is well within the abilities of any woodworker or hobbyist.

Adjustable shelving is made possible by the dozens of shelf pin styles now available.

Metal brackets of all shapes and sizes are used in the cabinet-making industry.

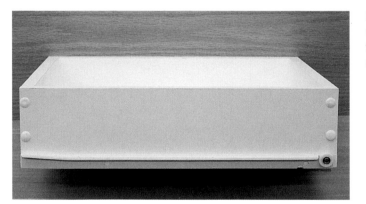

Bottom-mounted drawer guides simplify the drawer construction process.

Sheet Goods

Coated and plain particle core and ply-wood boards are stable materials that are suitable for many cabinet applications. These products are the most common building materials in today's furniture industry.

The melamine-coated decorative panels come in a wide range of colors. And best of all, they're already finished. The wood veneer boards can be stained, glued, joined and used like solid wood.

All of the colored panels and wood veneers have complementary edge tape that is attached with glue. In some cases, solid wood edging is installed to protect and accent the beauty of these boards.

High-Pressure Laminates

High-pressure laminates are the best materials for kitchen countertops. But there are many other cabinet applications.

I'll use some of these materials for the projects in this book and detail the installation procedures.

LIMITLESS POSSIBILITIES Modern sheet goods have opened many cabinet design possibilities.

EDGE TAPE Wood and melamine edge tapes are available for all the boards.

MELAMINE COLORS Dozens of decorative panel colors and textures are available.

LAMINATE COLORS High-pressure laminates are available in many colors.

CUTTING MELAMINE PB CHIP-FREE WITHOUT A TABLESAW

A table saw with a special melamine-cutting blade (called a triple-grind with carbide teeth) is the ideal tool when working with modern sheet goods. But you can get chip free cuts without a table saw.

A good circular saw, with a fine-toothed blade, will cut these boards cleanly if you follow a two-step process. A table saw chips melamine board on the underside during cutting, and the opposite is true for a radial arm saw. The blade rotation has a great deal to do with material damage.

To get a good cut with a circular saw, set the blade to cut 1/16" into your board. Clamp on a saw guide and make the first cut. Now, lower the blade until it's 1/16" deeper than the material thickness and make the final cut. It won't be perfect, but it will give you a reasonable cut.

If you want to achieve the perfect cut with veneers and melamine board, use a circular saw and a router.

Clamp a guide to the board and cut the material with your circular saw 1/8" longer than required. Next, install a carbide-tipped, straight cutting bit in your router. Set the guide so your router will cut off the 1/8" added length. Proceed slowly and hold the router firmly. You are cutting through glue and wood chips. The operation is noisy and dusty, so wear safety glasses, a dust mask and keep your hands firmly on the router.

The final cut will be clean and chip free. It takes a little extra time, but the results are worthwhile—perfect cuts everytime.

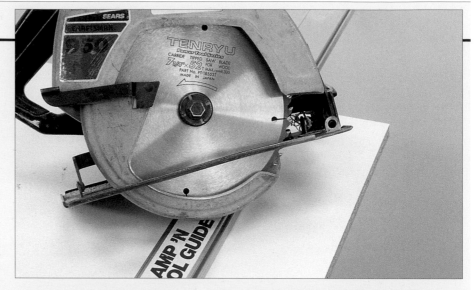

Particle board and wood veneer sheets can be successfully cut chip free without a table saw.

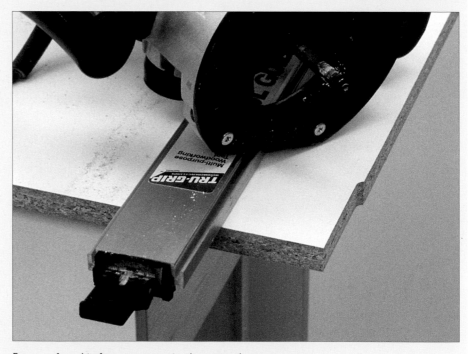

For a perfect chip-free cut, use a circular saw and a router.

INSTALLING DOORS WITH HIDDEN HINGES THE SIMPLE WAY

Door mounting jigs are available at all woodworking stores. If you plan to use the hidden hinge for many of your projects, these jigs are worthwhile.

If you're using the hidden hinge only occasionally, here's a quick and easy installation method without using a jig.

This method works with all hinge-mounting applications. It's based on using a 95° to 110° standard opening hinge. If you plan on installing a nonstandard hinge, such as the 170° model, install the door with a standard hinge boss mounted in the door, then replace the hinge boss with a 170° boss after the door has been hung.

First, drill the 35mm holes in the door and mount the hinge boss.

Secure the hinge boss in the hole, making certain it's at 90° to the door edge.

Attach the mounting plate to the hinge boss.

Place the door on the cabinet in its 90° open position. A $\frac{3}{16}$" thick spacer, between the door edge and the gable end edge, sets the correct door gap. Insert screws through the mounting plate to secure them to the cabinet side.

Doors with hidden hinges can be installed without jigs.

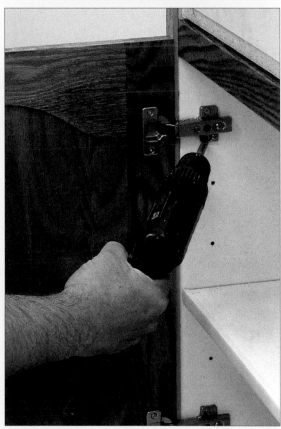

The proper door gap is set using a $\frac{3}{16}$" thick spacer. Secure the hinge plates with $\frac{5}{8}$" PB screws.

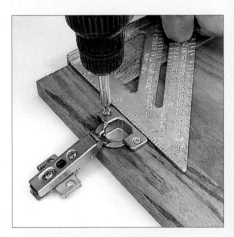

Align the mounting plate with a square before securing with screws.

CHAPTER 2
Home Work Center

Managing the household finances is a serious and time-consuming matter. Budgets, car payments, mortgage, as well as the normal monthly bills seem to generate loads of paper.

Many people file their bills in a kitchen cabinet or on top of the fridge until the month end. Then, it's a scramble to gather up all these documents, the calculator, files with previous statements, and the checkbook. All this material is carried to the kitchen table to be sorted out and paid. Well, this project just might be a way to organize that end-of-month rush and save you time as a bonus.

The home work center provides a great place to file documents in two 30"deep drawers. These full-extension drawers are designed to hold legal-size file folders. The compartment above will organize paper supplies, record books and computer accessories.

The desk is large and the return is designed for a computer workstation. A hutch above the desk has pigeonholes for computer disks and letters, and an adjustable shelf system for books.

This home work center is built using ⅝" particleboard with an English Oak pattern by PANOLAM. All the visible edges have a preglued, iron-on edge tape applied. I joined the panels using simple quick-connect hardware. Any joint that isn't visible is secured using 2" screws designed specifically for particleboard material.

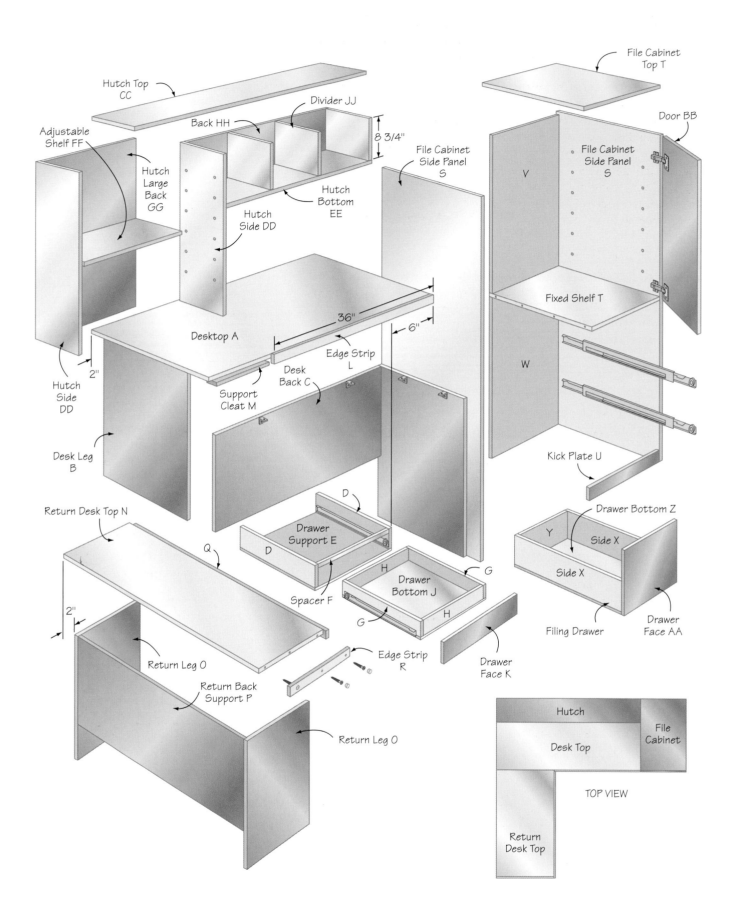

Building the Desk

The desk work surface can be any size. However, I've chosen the standard 30" × 60" size to meet my needs.

Applying the edge tape correctly is an acquired skill. Knowing how long to heat the tape, how much pressure when rolling and the art of trimming can be a little tricky. But it's not hard to become an expert. Practice with some scrap lumber until you're comfortable with the process. The one important technique is knowing how much heat to apply—too much and the glue runs from under the tape, too little and heat won't bond the tape properly.

The edge tape is available in large rolls. A 100' roll should be more than enough to complete the project. Follow the instructions supplied by the manufacturer.

REQUIRED TOOLS

Table or circular saw

Drill

Jigsaw or band saw

T-square jig

Combination square

Hammer

Nail set

Sander (or sandpaper and block)

Cutting List • Desk

REF.	QTY.	PART	STOCK	THICK	WIDTH	LENGTH	COMMENTS
A	1	Desktop	Veneer PB	$\frac{5}{8}$	29 $\frac{1}{4}$	60	
B	2	Legs	Veneer PB	$\frac{5}{8}$	26	29 $\frac{3}{8}$	
C	1	Back Support	Veneer PB	$\frac{5}{8}$	18	58	
D	2	Drawer Support Side	Veneer PB	$\frac{5}{8}$	5	22	
E	1	Drawer Support Bottom	Veneer PB	$\frac{5}{8}$	22	24	
F	2	Spacers	Veneer PB	$\frac{5}{8}$	1 $\frac{1}{2}$	22 $\frac{3}{4}$	
G	2	Drawer Sides	BalticBirch	$\frac{1}{2}$	2 $\frac{1}{4}$	22	
H	2	Drawer Front and Back	BalticBirch	$\frac{1}{2}$	2 $\frac{1}{4}$	20 $\frac{3}{4}$	
J	1	Drawer Bottom	BalticBirch	$\frac{1}{4}$	21 $\frac{3}{4}$	22	
K	1	Drawer Face	Veneer PB	$\frac{5}{8}$	4 $\frac{1}{2}$	24	
L	1	Wood Edge	Hardwood	$\frac{3}{4}$	1 $\frac{1}{2}$	36	
M	1	Support Cleat	Veneer PB	$\frac{3}{4}$	3 $\frac{1}{2}$	23	

Hardware & Supplies

	1 Set	22" Bottom-Mounted Drawer Glides
		Matching Edge Tape
		Carpenter's Glue
		Quick Connect Hardware
		Right Angle Brackets
		1 $\frac{1}{2}$" Spiral Finishing Nails
		$\frac{5}{8}$", 1" and 2" PB Screws
		$\frac{3}{8}$" Wooden Plugs
	1	Drawer Handle

1 After cutting the desktop A to size and taping the left edge only, cut the two leg panels B to size and apply edge tape to both 29⅜" edges. Mount the leg panels 2" from the front edge of the desk top with two #40.200 style connector made by BLUM. (You can also use angle brackets with screws if you prefer.) Make sure that the right side is flush with the top's edge, and the left is 2" in from the top's edge.

2 Cut the back support panel C and apply edge tape to the left 18" end. Use 2" particleboard (PB) screws to attach the panel to the legs. Add two more connectors to secure the support panel to the underside of the desktop.

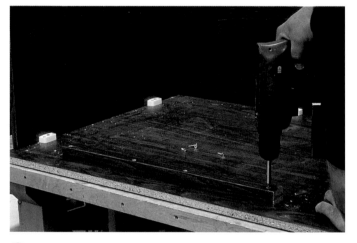

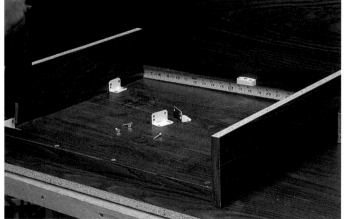

3 Cut the drawer spacers F to size and apply tape to one 22¾" edge on each spacer. Attach the spacers to the underside of the desktop, 2" back from the front edge and 6⅝" in from the right end, with the taped edge facing forward. Use 1" screws to secure one spacer under the desk top and four more 1" screws to attach the second spacer on top of the first.

4 Install the side panels D to the desktop with right angle brackets and ⅝" screws. The taped ends should be facing forward and flush with the spacer boards. The outside face of the side boards should be 24" apart.

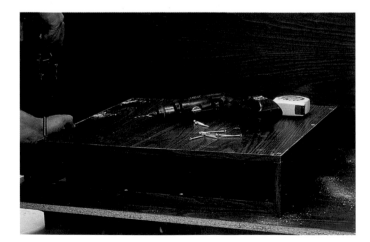

5 Drill pilot holes and attach the drawer compartment bottom E with its taped edge forward with 2" PB screws.

6 Cut all the drawer box parts G, H and J from Baltic Birch as detailed in the materials list and sand the edges smooth. Since the bottom-mounted drawer glides I use require ½" per side for proper operation, my drawer box is 1" narrower than the opening. Normally, my drawer box height is also 1" less. Attach the side boards G to the front and back H using glue and 1½" spiral finishing nails.

7 Glue and nail the bottom board J to the sides, front and back to complete the drawer box.

TIP *Mounting drawer fronts accurately can be difficult. But there is an easy method. First, drill the handle holes. Then, hold the drawer face in position and drive screws through the handle holes into the drawer box. Remove the drawer with the face attached and secure the face from the rear. Finally, remove the screws and install your handle hardware.*

8 Install the 22" bottom-mounted drawer glides according to the instructions with your hardware.

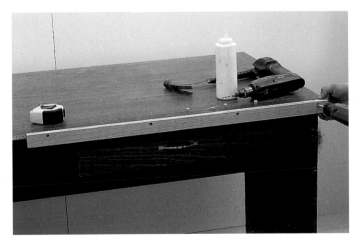

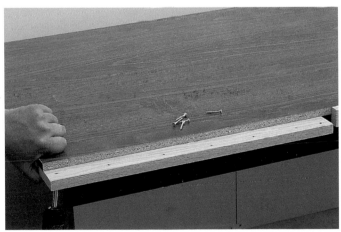

9 Tape all the edges of the drawer face K and align the bottom with the lower surface of the drawer compartment frame. Align the solid wood edge L with the right hand side of the desktop and then attach it to the desktop with glue and 2" screws in counterbored holes. Fill the holes with wood plugs (This solid wood strip will protect the desk where chairs will likely hit the edge.)

10 Make a support cleat M as detailed in the materials list and attach it to the left side of the desk. Use 1¼" screws and leave half the board extended out front.

Building the Return

The return top is 23¼" × 44¼", with the long back edge taped.

Materials List • Return

REF.	QTY.	PART	STOCK	THICK	WIDTH	LENGTH	COMMENTS
N	1	Return Top	Veneer PB	⅝	23¼	44¼	
O	2	Leg Panels	Veneer PB	⅝	20	29⅜	
P	1	Back Support	Veneer PB	⅝	18	40¼	
Q	1	Edge Strip	Hardwood	¾	1½	45	
R	1	Edge Strip	Hardwood	¾	1½	23¼	

Hardware & Supplies

		Matching Edge Tape
		2" PB Screws
	1	Computer Keyboard Pull-Out Tray
	2	Grommets
		Blum Connectors
		⅜" Wood Plugs

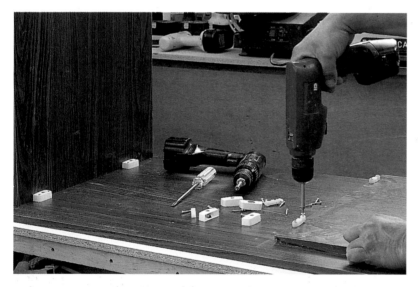

1 Cut the leg panels O and tape both long edges on each panel. Then attach the legs to the underside of the return top N using the connectors. (Each leg is 2" in from the back edge and 2" in from the return's ends.)

2 Cut the return's back support P and tape both ends. Use 2" screws to attach the support to the legs and two connectors to anchor the return top and support.

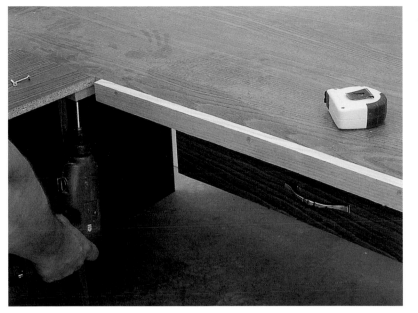

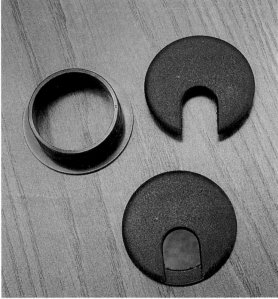

3 Temporarily attach the return to the desk with screws through the wood support cleat M. The return's back should be flush with the desktop's left end.

4 Drill holes on each end of the return to allow for the computer cables, and install the grommets.

5 Attach the two wood edge strips Q and R to the front and side of the return with glue and 2" screws in counterbored holes that can be filled with ⅜" wood plugs. Make sure the top surfaces of the strips are flush with the return's top.

6 Use a belt sander to ease the corner where the strips meet to prevent injury should someone bump into the corner. Then with a ⅜" router bit or sandpaper, round over the top and bottom edges of the wood strip. Apply masking tape to the area where the router will travel to prevent it from scratching the desktop.

Building the Legal-Size File Cabinet

Materials List • Legal-Size File Cabinet

REF.	QTY.	PART	STOCK	THICK	WIDTH	LENGTH	COMMENTS
S	2	Side Panels	Veneer PB	⅝	30	58	
T	2	Fixed Shelves	Veneer PB	⅝	17½	30	
U	1	Kickplate	Veneer PB	⅝	2	17½	
V	1	Top Back Board	Veneer PB	⅝	17½	26¾	
W	1	Bottom Back Board	Veneer PB	⅝	17½	30	
X	4	Drawer Sides	BalticBirch	½	8	28	
Y	4	Fronts and Backs	BalticBirch	½	8	15½	
Z	2	Bottoms	BalticBirch	½	16½	28	
AA	2	Drawer Fronts	Veneer PB	⅝	18½	14½	
BB	1	Door	Veneer PB	⅝	18½	27½	
	2	Adjustable Shelves	Veneer PB	⅝	17⁷⁄₁₆	29¼	

Hardware & Supplies

2	28" Full-Extension Drawer Glides	
	2" Particleboard Screws	
	Quick-Connectors and Right-Angle Brackets	
	1½" Spiral Finishing Nails	
2	Hidden Hinges	
	Matching Edge Tape	
8	Shelf Pins	
3	Drawer Pulls	

1 Cut the two side panels S and tape one long edge, which will be the front, and one short edge, which is the top. Prepare the two fixed shelves T by taping one 17½" edge, which is the front. Then with quick-lock connectors, join one shelf to the sides flush with the top edge, and one shelf 30" up from the bottom.

2 Install the kick plate U with one quick-connector per side at the bottom front of the file cabinet.

3 Install the top and bottom back boards V and W flush with the back edge of the file cabinet box. Use quick connectors on top and right angle brackets on the bottom. (File drawers will hide the bottom panel.)

4 Construct a drill jig that's 24" high with holes spaced 2" apart. Drill two columns of holes on the inside of each panel S to support shelf pins. (Use a dowel rod or drill stop to limit the bit travel.) The hole size depends on which shelf pin you've chosen. Then cut and test-fit the adjustable shelves.

5 Build the legal-size drawers from ½" Baltic Birch. The rule in step six in the desk instructions regarding side clearance applies when using full-extension glides: ½" space on each side of the drawer box. Follow the same steps as you performed in building the desk drawer.

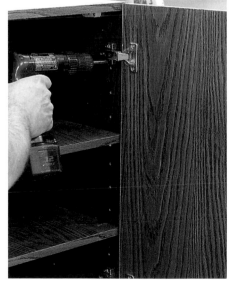

6 Attach the full-extension 28" drawer glides following the manufacturer's installation instructions. It doesn't matter which drawer glide hardware you use as long as the bottom drawer's top edge is 12" above the cabinet bottom. The top drawer must be 26" above the cabinet bottom. (These dimensions are needed to accommodate the drawer faces.)

7 Tape all edges on the two drawer faces AA, and then install the faces, with the bottom drawer face 1" above the floor and a ⅟₁₆" space left between the two drawer faces.

8 Cut the door BB to size, tape all the edges and install the door using hidden hinges following the steps outlined in chapter one.

Materials List • Hutch

REF.	QTY.	PART	STOCK	THICK	WIDTH	LENGTH	COMMENTS
CC	1	Top	Veneer PB	⅝	10	60	
DD	2	Sides	Veneer PB	⅝	10	27⅛	
EE	1	Bottom	Veneer PB	⅝	10	36	
FF	2	Shelves	Veneer PB	⅝	10	22¹¹⁄₁₆	
GG	1	Back	Veneer PB	⅝"	24	27¾	
HH	1	Back	Veneer PB	⅝"	10	36	
JJ	3	Dividers	Veneer PB	⅝"	10	8¾	

Hardware & Supplies

		Quick-Connectors and Right-Angle Brackets
		Screws with Decorative Caps
		Matching Edge Tape
		2" Particleboard Screws
	8	Shelf Pins
		Wood Stain and/or Polyurathane Finish

Building the Hutch

The hutch panels are joined with a decorative screw that has threads inside the head. Once the screw is inserted flush with the panel surface, a screw-on cover cap is attached. A number of different styles of these screws is available, so choose one that matches the handles on your center.

After cutting your parts to size, there are some special areas to pay attention to when applying your tape. First, the top board CC should have one long and one short edge taped, while the two long book case side panels DD should have one long edge taped on each board. The lower shelf section EE should have just one long edge taped, and the three dividers JJ should have tape applied to one 8¾" edge on each panel. The bookcase back has to be taped on both long edges and

one short edge (which will be the top), and the divider section back needs both long edges taped.

After taping is finished, assemble the hutch as shown in the technical drawing. Use screws with decorative caps in all areas that will be visible. Attach the bookcase back and the divider section back using 2" particleboard screws. Then with the shelf-hole jig, drill the holes for the bookcase section of the hutch.

Secure the hutch to the desk with screws from the underside of the desktop. Attach the other end of the hutch to the file cabinet with two screws from inside the cabinet's upper section. Finally, stain the wood edge to match the decorative board, or simply cover the wood with three coats of polyurethane as I did.

CONSTRUCTION OPTIONS

It isn't necessary to build your work center with decorative panels—this is one option that I've shown. You can use inexpensive medium density fiberboard, PB, or even good two-sided plywood and paint the unit.

You might also want to use the less-expensive right angle brackets in place of the connectors. These brackets can be painted a color closely matching the material you choose.

Customize the size to fit your needs. None of these dimensions are cast in stone. Make the return shorter or longer, change the hutch, or alter the file cabinet height. The choice is yours.

And finally, I've shown the simplest joinery method. If you are comfortable with plate or dowel joinery, use those methods. If you like dovetail-jointed drawers, use that system. In short, build the center with any joinery system based on your knowledge and equipment.

Common Adhesives

ADHESIVE	ADVANTAGES	DISADVANTAGES	COMMON USES	WORKING TIME	CLAMPING TIME (at 70° F)	CURE TIME	SOLVENT
Yellow glue (aliphatic resin)	Easy to use; water resistant; water cleanup; economical.	Not waterproof (don't use on outdoor furniture).	All-purpose wood glue for interior use; stronger bond than white glue.	5 to 7 minutes.	1 to 2 hours.	24 hours.	Warm water.
Contact cement	Bonds parts immediately.	Can't readjust parts after contact.	Bonding veneer or plastic laminate to substrate.	Up to 1 hour.	No clamps; parts bond on contact.	None.	Acetone.
Superglue (Cyanoacrylate)	Bonds parts quickly.	Limited to small parts.	Bonding small parts made from a variety of materials.	30 seconds.	10 to 60 seconds; clamps usually not required.	30 minutes to several hours.	Acetone.
Epoxy glue	Good gap filler; waterproof; fast-setting formulas available; can be used to bond glass to metal or wood.	Requires mixing.	Bonding small parts made from a variety of materials.	5 to 60 minutes depending on epoxy formula.	5 minutes to several hours depending on epoxy formula.	3 hours or longer.	Lacquer thinner.
Animal glue, dry (hide glue)	Extended working time; water cleanup; economical.	Must be mixed with water and heated; poor moisture resistance (don't use on outdoor furniture).	Time-consuming assembly work; stronger bond than liquid animal glue; interior use only.	30 minutes.	2 to 3 hours.	24 hours.	Warm water.
Animal glue, liquid (hide glue)	Easy to use; extended working time; water cleanup; economical.	Poor moisture resistance (don't use on outdoor furniture).	Time-consuming assembly work; interior use only.	5 minutes.	2 hours.	24 hours.	Warm water.
Polyurethane	Fully waterproof; gap-filling.	Eye and skin irritant.	Interior and exterior applications including wood to wood, ceramic, plastic, Corian, stone, metal.	30 minutes.	1 to 2 hours.	8 hours.	Mineral spirits while wet; must abrade or scrape off when dry.
White glue (polyvinyl acetate)	Easy to use; economical.	Not waterproof (don't use on outdoor furniture).	All-purpose wood glue for interior use; yellow glue has stronger bond.	3 to 5 minutes.	16 hours.	24 to 48 hours.	Warm water and soap.
Waterproof glue (resorcinol)	Fully waterproof; extended working time.	Requires mixing; dark color shows glue line on most woods; long clamping time.	Outdoor furniture, marine applications.	20 minutes.	1 hour.	12 hours.	Cool water before hardening.
Plastic resin (urea formaldehyde)	Good water resistance; economical.	Requires mixing; long clamping time.	Outdoor furniture, cutting boards.	15 to 30 minutes.	6 hours.	24 hours.	Warm water and soap before hardening.

CHAPTER 3

Child's Closet Work Center

Many children's bedrooms never have enough space. The bed and dresser usually take up a great deal of the floor space, leaving little room for a desk. However, the closets in these rooms have been designed for adult clothes, such as long dresses, suits and shirts, not for the types of clothing you'd find in a young child's wardrobe. Since most of their clothes can be easily kept in a dresser, why not turn the closet into a work/storage center!

This project has a small cabinet for hanging dress clothes, and many shelves and drawers that can be used for either toy or clothes storage. All the shelves are adjustable, so just about any storage problem you have can be accommodated.

The highlight of the center is a desk area for play and study time. And three sturdy shelves above the desk to hold books.

This project is made of oak veneer particleboard (PB). All the joinery is done with glue and screws designed for PB. If the screws will be visible, the holes are counterbored and an oak wood button is installed.

In this project, I'll detail a drawer design made with melamine-coated PB, how to install high-pressure laminates for a great-looking desk surface, and how to join solid wood to PB.

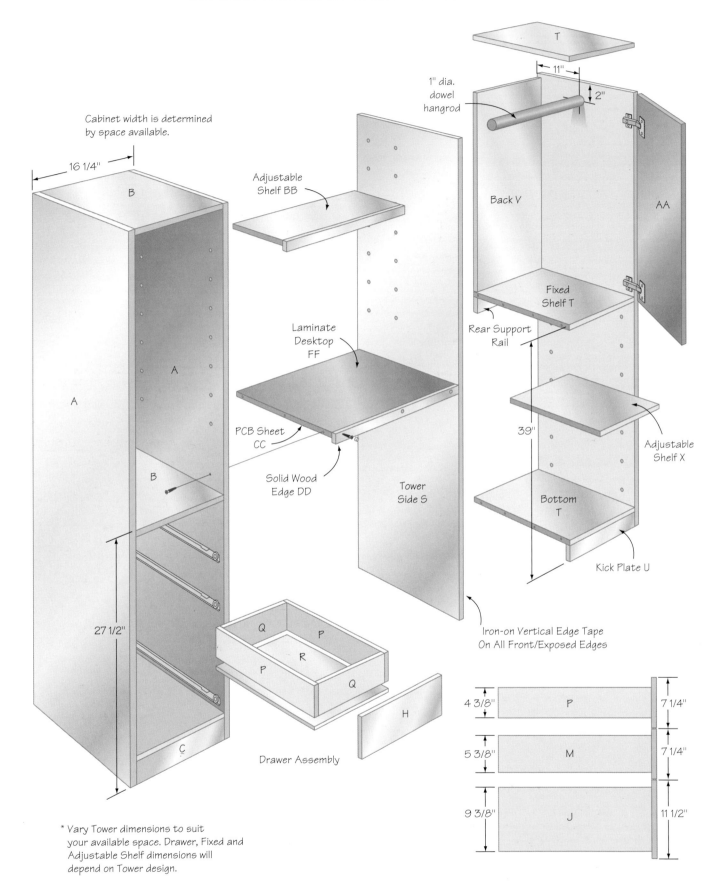

Cabinet width is determined
by space available.

16 1/4"

1" dia.
dowel
hangrod

11"

2"

B

Adjustable
Shelf BB

Back V

AA

T

A

A

Laminate
Desktop
FF

Fixed
Shelf T

Rear Support
Rail

A

PCB Sheet
CC

B

Solid Wood
Edge DD

Tower
Side S

39"

Adjustable
Shelf X

27 1/2"

Bottom
T

Kick Plate U

Q

P

R

P

Q

Iron-on Vertical Edge Tape
On All Front/Exposed Edges

C

H

Drawer Assembly

4 3/8"

P

7 1/4"

5 3/8"

M

7 1/4"

9 3/8"

J

11 1/2"

* Vary Tower dimensions to suit
your available space. Drawer, Fixed and
Adjustable Shelf dimensions will
depend on Tower design.

Materials List • Child's Closet Work Center

REF.	QTY.	PART	STOCK	THICK	WIDTH	LENGTH	COMMENTS
Left Tower							
A	2	Tower sides	Veneer PB	¾	23	72	
B	2	Fixed shelves	Veneer PB	¾	14¾	23	
C	1	Kickplate	Veneer PB	¾	2	14¾	
D	1	Back Panel	Veneer PB	¾	14¾	26¾	
E	1	Rear rail	Veneer PB	¾	2	14¾	
F	4	Shelves	Veneer PB	¾	14¹¹⁄₁₆	23	
G	1	Drawer front	Veneer PB	¾	11½	15¾	
H	2	Drawer fronts	Veneer PB	¾	7¼	15¾	
Drawers							
J	2	Sides	Coated PB	⅝	9⅜	22	
K	2	Backs & fronts	Coated PB	⅝	9⅜	12½	
L	1	Bottom	Coated PB	⅝	13¾	22	
M	2	Sides	Coated PB	⅝	5⅜	22	
N	2	Backs & fronts	Coated PB	⅝	5⅜	12½	
O	1	Bottom	Coated PB	⅝	13¾	22	
P	2	Sides	Coated PB	⅝	4⅜	22	
Q	2	Back & front	Coated PB	⅝	4⅜	12½	
R	1	Bottom	Coated PB	⅝	13¾	22	
Right Tower							
S	2	Tower sides	Veneer PB	¾	23	72	
T	3	Fixed shelves	Veneer PB	¾	17	23	
U	1	Kickplate	Veneer PB	¾	2	17	
V	1	Back board	Veneer PB	¾	17	32¼	
W	1	Rear rail	Veneer PB	¾	2	17	
X	4	Shelves	Veneer PB	¾	16¹⁵⁄₁₆	23	
AA	1	Door	Veneer PB	¾	18	33½	
Middle Section							
BB	3	Shelves	Veneer PB	¾	9	28¼	
CC	1	Sheet	PB	¾	22	28¼	
DD	1	Wood edge	Hardwood	¾	1½	28¼	
EE	2	Mounting cleats	Hardwood	¾	¾	22	
FF	1	Desktop surface	HP-Lam	¾	24	30	
	3	Wood edges	Hardwood	¾	1½	28¼	

Hardware & Supplies

	1¼", 1½", and 2" PB Screws		White Plastic Screw Caps
3	Drawer Pulls		Wood Buttons
3 sets	22" Bottom-Mounted Drawer Glides		Wood Veneer Edge Tape
1	17" x 1" Dia. Wood Dowel		White Edge Tape
2	Hidden Hinges		Carpenter's Glue
16	Plastic Covered Steel Shelf Pins		

REQUIRED TOOLS

Table or circular saw

Jigsaw or band saw

T-square jig

Combination square

Hammer and Nail set

Iron

Router

Drill

JOINERY POSSIBILITIES

The joinery possibilities for this project are numerous. However, I will be using a simple butt joint that's secured with glue and 2" particleboard (PB) screws. When the screws are installed on a visible face, I have counterbored the screw hole at a ⅜"-diameter, which allows me to glue a wood button in place. It's a strong and simple joint.

Building the Work Center

1 Cut the four tower sides A and S and apply edge tape to one long edge on each. (I used ¹³⁄₁₆" oak veneer edge tape that is pre-glued and heat-activated with a household iron.)

2 Cut the two fixed left tower shelves B and tape one 14¾" edge on each shelf. Attach one fixed shelf flush with the top edge of the two left-tower sides A. Attach the second fixed shelf so its top surface is 27½" above the tower panel's bottom edge. Cut and install a 2"-high kick plate C to the bottom front face of the tower, and apply tape to the top edge. Then install the left-tower back panel D behind the drawer bank. (All the backs on this project are set in flush with the back edge of the tower.) Use glue and three screws per side. Apply a little glue to the top edge of this panel so it will bond with the middle fixed shelf and stiffen the tower.

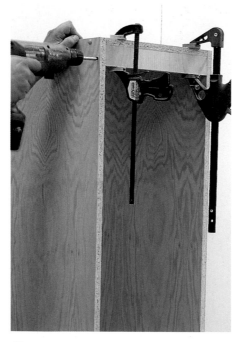

3 tape the bottom long edge only of the upper rear rail E and install it in the left tower,

4 With a shelf hole jig 4" x 40" drill the holes for the shelf pins in the upper section of the tower. Use a small dowel drilled through the center as a drill stop, to keep from accidentally drilling through the cabinet.

Building the Drawers

I have used ⅝" thick melamine coated PB for my drawers. It's a tough material and is easily wiped clean.

1 After cutting all the parts J through R for the three drawers to size, apply white edge tape to all top edges of the sides, backs, and fronts, as well as the long sides of the bottom boards. Then assemble the drawer boxes by attaching side boards to the fronts and backs with 2" PB screws and white plastic screw head caps.

2 Install the bottom boards with 2" screws in piloted holes, 6" apart.

3 Install the drawer hardware according to the manufacturer's directions. (For this project, I used 22" bottom mounted drawer glides.)

4 Mount the carcass runners in the cabinet. The tracks are located 2¾", 14", and 21" from the tower's bottom edge.

5 Test-fit the drawer boxes. Once their proper operation is verified, cut and tape all the drawer face edges. Then locate and install the drawer faces G and H from the top down. Align the top face with the upper surface of the middle fixed shelf, and space the drawer fronts ¹⁄₁₆" apart, using the handle holes to temporarily secure the front. Drive two 1¼" screws from inside the box into the fronts, and then install the drawer pulls.

TIP *Some species of wood veneer edge tapes tend to split along the grain when trimmed. Oak, because of its wide grain structure, is one that tears easily. Because of these qualities, it is easy to ruin your veneer when sanding with a power sander. Go slowly, use a fine-grit paper, and make light passes. Practice with some scrap wood until you get the proper feel for this procedure.*

Building the Right Tower

2 Install a rear support rail W in the right tower with glue, 2" PB screws and wood buttons on the visible side.

1 Join the last two tower sides S to the fixed shelves T, one shelf is attached flush with the top edge of both sides: the other is located 39" from its upper surface to the top edge of the tower sides. Then install a 2" high front kick plate. (You don't have to tape any edges on this piece because a fixed bottom shelf will be fitted covering the top edge.)

3 Install the right tower back panel V in the upper section to form a closet for hanging clothes. Attach the back so its back face is flush with the tower's back edges.

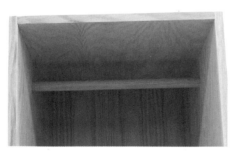

5 Cut the four adjustable right-tower shelves X, tape one short edge on each and test-fit. Then install a 1" diameter wood rod for clothes. Position the rod 11" back from the front edge and 2" down from the top fixed shelf, and secure it with glue and 2" screws through the outer face of each tower side.

4 Drill holes for adjustable pins in the lower section of the right tower.

6 Cut out the door AA and tape all edges. Follow the procedures detailed in Chapter one for installing the hidden hinges.

Making a Desktop

The desktop is made with ¾" PB. A wood edge is attached and sanded flush with the PB surface. High-pressure laminate is then attached with contact cement. Both the laminate and edging are then cut with a router to create a profile.

This isn't a critical design element, so just about any flat surfaced material can be used for the top. Most home stores carry wood panels that are ideal for this application.

1 After cutting a piece of ¾" PB or plywood to the finished size, glue and screw a wood edge DD to the front using screws in piloted holes. Counterbore the holes before installing the screws as they will be filled with wood plugs. Then sand smooth.

2 To stiffen the top and give the installation screws more hold, increase the PB edge with ¾" square solid wood cleats EE. Use glue and 1 ¼" long screws in pre-drilled pilot holes to ensure maximum grip.

3 Cut a piece of high pressure laminate FF for the desktop 1" larger in both directions than needed. Apply contact cement, and once it is set, lay the laminate carefully on the desktop. Roll the surface flat beginning in the center and working toward the edges. Then with a flush trim bit and your router, trim away the excess laminate.

4 Soften the bottom front edge of the wood trim with a ⅜" roundover bit in a router. To produce a clean, straight edge on the desk top, set the roundover bit low enough so the straight wings cut slightly lower than the laminate's thickness on the desktop edge. (The cut is approximately ¹⁄₁₆" below the laminate.)

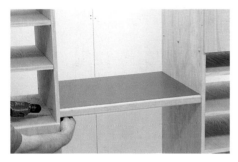

5 Install the desktop between the two towers so the top surface is 30" above the floor. Use four 1 ½" screws per side from inside both towers and screw into the solid wood cleats under the top.

Building and Installing the Adjustable Bookshelves

These shelves will carry a great deal of weight if they are loaded with books. So it's important that both towers be anchored to the wall. The shelves have a 1 × 2 screwed and glued to the front edge for added shelf strength, and I've used plastic covered steel pins to support my shelves. They should be able to support a great deal of weight by building them in this way.

After cutting the ¾" veneer PB shelves BB to length as detailed in the materials list, attach a solid wood edge with glue and screws in counterbored pilot holes. Fill the holes with wood plugs. Then soften the front edge with either a ⅜" roundover bit in your router or with sandpaper.

Use the shelf-hole jig to drill the tower sides. I adjusted the size of my jig and raised it off the desktop to drill the pin holes. Then install the shelf pins and verify that all the shelves fit properly.

WORKING WITH CONTACT CEMENT

Contact cements set up immediately, and it is important to cut the piece you are gluing 1" larger in both directions than you need to simplify the positioning after the contact cement has been applied. This adhesive permits only one try. Once the two surfaces touch, you cannot reposition the laminate.

Contact adhesive's fumes can be dangerous so it's well worth the time to read and understand the instructions supplied with the product you plan to use. Pay attention to the safety rules as well as the environmental conditions necessary for a successful application. Heat and humidity can affect drying times of this adhesive.

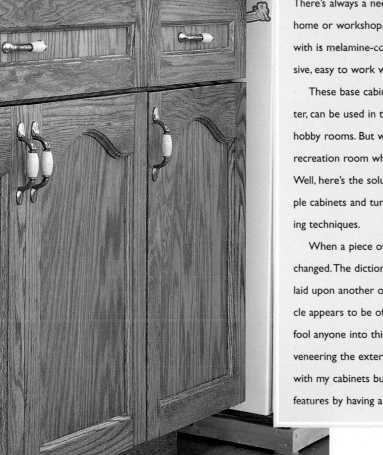

CHAPTER 4

Utility Base Cabinets

There's always a need for simple, functional cabinets around the home or workshop. The most popular sheet material to build with is melamine-coated particleboard (PB). It's stable, inexpensive, easy to work with and, best of all, doesn't require painting.

These base cabinets, and the wall cabinets in the next chapter, can be used in the workshop, laundry room, basement and hobby rooms. But what about using them in an area like the recreation room where something a little fancier is required? Well, here's the solution. I'll show you how to build these simple cabinets and turn them into elegant cabinetry using veneering techniques.

When a piece of material is veneered, the look is drastically changed. The dictionary defines *veneer* as "a thin piece of wood laid upon another of a less valuable sort, so that the whole article appears to be of a more valuable sort". I'm not trying to fool anyone into thinking I'm building a solid oak cabinet by veneering the exterior. However, I want a more formal look with my cabinets but I also want to retain the low maintenance features by having a melamine PB interior.

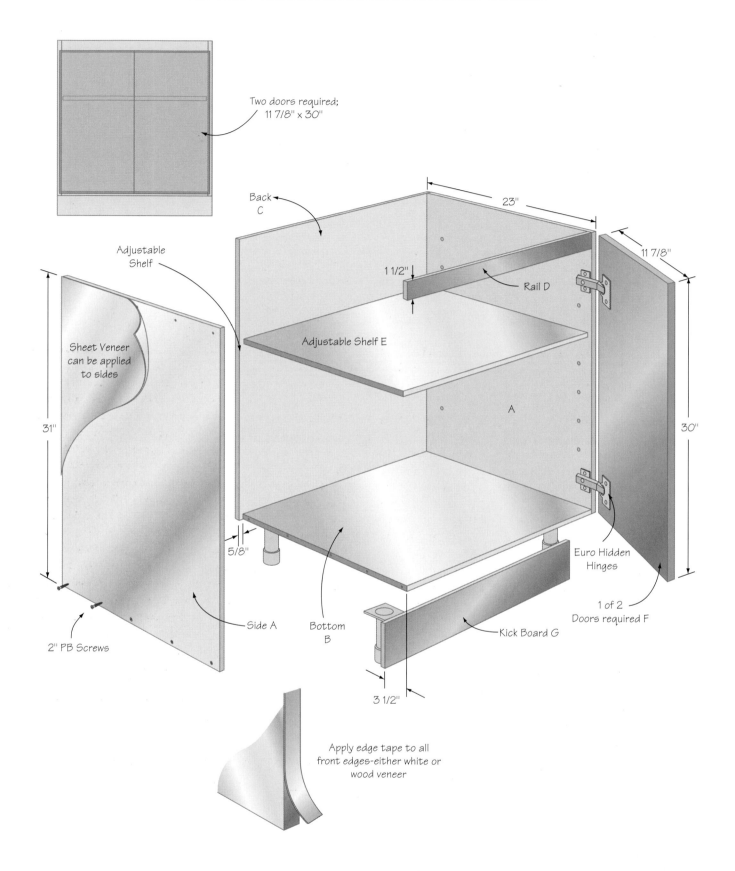

Two doors required;
11 7/8" x 30"

Back
C

23"

Adjustable
Shelf

11 7/8"

1 1/2"

Rail D

Sheet Veneer
can be applied
to sides

Adjustable Shelf E

A

31"

30"

5/8"

Euro Hidden
Hinges

2" PB Screws

Side A

Bottom
B

Kick Board G

1 of 2
Doors required F

3 1/2"

Apply edge tape to all
front edges-either white or
wood veneer

Materials List • Utility Base Cabinets

REF.	QTY.	PART	STOCK	THICK	WIDTH	LENGTH	COMMENTS
A	2	Sides	Coated PB	⅝	23	31	
B	1	Bottom	Coated PB	⅝	23	22¾	
C	1	Back	Coated PB	⅝	24	31	
D	1	Rail	Coated PB	⅝	1½	22¾	
E	1	Shelf	Coated PB	⅝	22⅝	231	
F	2	Doors	Coated PB	⅝	11⅞	30⅛	
G	1	Kick	Coated PB	⅝	3½	24	

Hardware & Supplies

4	Cabinet legs		Matching Edge Tape
4	Shelf Pins		Countertop clips and Kick Board Clips
4	Hidden Hinges		⅝" and 2" PB Screws

Frameless Base Cabinet Basics

The basic frameless base cabinet is a box with two sides, called gable ends, a bottom board, and a back panel. There is normally a door or door-and-drawer combination with fixed or adjustable shelving inside the cabinet.

Base cabinets differ from wall cabinets because they are on legs or a platform. Therefore the exposed side legs or base frame must be inset 3½" to allow for a toe kick board.

Frameless base cabinets require an upper rail so the door clears the countertop. For my cabinets, I use a 1½"-high rail. Its height is constant regardless of the cabinet width, and its width is equal to the bottom board's width.

All base cabinets are not the same width. We often need cabinets of a specific width to fill dedicated spaces. Standard utility base cabinets are 36" high when complete. That height accounts for the cabinet base support and the countertop thickness. For these cabinets, I will be using plastic adjustable legs, but you can construct a wood base just as easily. The following chart lists all the box or carcase parts needed to build a frameless base cabinet using ⅝" melamine PB.

Material Thickness

Not all material is actually ⅝" thick. Variances can occur from the manufacturer. Some produce a 16mm board while others make a true ⅝"-thick board. But it's not a serious issue except when cutting the back panel. Verify the actual thickness of the material you are using and cut the back width accordingly. You may have to add a $\frac{1}{32}$" or possibly a $\frac{1}{16}$" to the width.

Custom Cabinet Widths

You may need a cabinet width that's not on the chart for your specific application. That isn't a problem. If, for example, I required a 31½" wide base cabinet, I would have to cut the back 31½" wide and the bottom 30¼" wide. All other dimensions remain the same. The door, upper rail and shelf widths would have to change, but they are easily calculated, as you'll see when we construct the cabinet.

CALCULATING DOOR SIZE

Cabinets without a face frame, commonly called frameless style, are best fitted with doors using full-overlay hidden hinges. But it can be tricky to determine the door size when using these hinges. If you determine your dimensions as shown in the following example, you'll never run into trouble.

Let's say your cabinet box is 31" high, with a 1½" high rail. A 24" wide cabinet has an inside width of 22¾" which is the bottom's width. The door, or doors on a double door cabinet, should be 1" wider in total than the interior width. Therefore, you would need two 11⅞"-wide doors. Since the door is mounted flush with the bottom surface of the bottom board and overlaps the rail by ½", you would need a door height of 30".

So in general, doors are 1" wider than the inside cabinet width, and 1" lower than the cabinet sides when using a 1½"-high upper rail.

Calculating Cabinet Width

CABINET WIDTH	TWO SIDES D × H	ONE BOTTOM D × W	ONE BACK W × H
12"	23" × 31"	23" × 10¾"	12" × 31"
15"	23" × 31"	23" × 13¾"	15" × 31"
18"	23" × 31"	23" × 16¾"	18" × 31"
21"	23" × 31"	23" × 19¾"	21" × 31"
24"	23" × 31"	23" × 22¾"	24" × 31"
27"	23" × 31"	23" × 25¾"	27" × 31"
30"	23" × 31"	23" × 28¾"	30" × 31"
33"	23" × 31"	23" × 31¾"	33" × 31"
36"	23" × 31"	23" × 34¾"	36" × 31"

WORKING WITH PARTICLEBOARD

Most professional cabinetmakers use a cabinet-grade melamine coated particleboard. Particleboard is formed with glue and wood particles. The melamine surface is a paper coating that has been soaked in resin and bonded to the board to make it scratch resistant.

Three main grades are available: 100, 120 and 140. I prefer the 120-grade board. There are some less expensive melamine PB on the market, and while they seem like a good buy, they are more likely to scratch and break. The particles are coarse and the glue is poor. Ask for cabinet grade-material when purchasing these sheet goods.

The high glue content of this board makes it very hard, and as many people who use high-speed steel tools have discovered, it can ruin a saw blade or tool bit quickly. It's therefore a wise investment to use carbide-tipped cutting tools when working with this material.

Additionally, screws will hold properly only if the board has been predrilled. A hole will allow the screw to cut a thread and grip very tightly. Without a pilot hole, the boards will split.

There is a special screw for particleboard joinery. The shaft is thin and the threads are coarse. This allows the screw to cut a deep, well-defined threaded hole, forming an amazingly tight joint.

TIP *Leave your boards about ¼" longer than needed. After applying the edge tape, cut ⅛" off each end. That will leave you with perfectly trimmed edge-tape ends.*

Building a 24" Frameless Base Cabinet

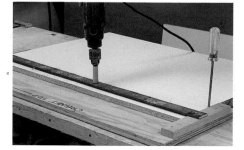

1 Cut all the parts as detailed in the materials list. With a shelf-hole jig, drill holes for the adjustable shelf pins. These jigs are not elaborate things, just a piece of flat metal mounted on two ¾" blocks that are 31 1/16" apart. Shelf-hole spacing is a matter of personal taste; however, I normally space them 1½" on center.

3 Secure the bottom B to the sides A with 2" PB screws. Space the screws 6" apart and always pre-drill and countersink the screw hole. Then attach the back with 2" PB screws at 6" centers. Ensure that the back is flush with the bottom edge of the bottom and flush with the outside edges of the sides.

REQUIRED TOOLS

Table or circular saw

Jigsaw or band saw

T-Square jig

Combination square

Hammer

Nail set

Router

Drill

Screwdrivers

Iron

2 Apply edge tape to the exposed edges of the sides, bottom and underside of the top rail. The easiest tape to apply is heat-activated with an iron. Use an inexpensive hand trimmer to remove the excess tape on the sides.

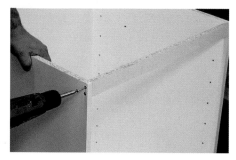

4 Secure the rail D to the base cabinet using 2" screws. Install two screws per side in predrilled pilot holes.

TIP *I use the 1½" high rail for a specific reason. When I veneer my cabinets, I replace the melamine PB rail with solid wood to match the veneer. And since the 1½" height is the dressed size of 1x2 boards, I simply cut my rail lengths from this standard wood size.*

TIP *A hinge is properly installed when it's at 90° to the door's edge. Use a square to align the hinge when inserting the screws.*

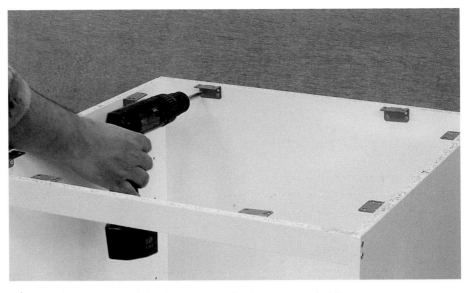

5 Attach four adjustable legs, one per corner, 3½" back from the front edge. Secure them with ⅝" PB screws so they support the sides.

6 With ⅝" PB screws, install eight countertop brackets, two per inside face, on the side, back and rail boards.

7 Tape the doors F with white iron-on edge tape. Drill two 35mm holes in each door, ⅛" back from the door edge and 4" on center from the bottom and top. These holes will be used to attach the hidden hinges.

8 Screw the hinges in place with the cabinet hinge plate attached. (I am using Blum 107°clip-on full overlay hinges on my cabinet.)

9 A kick board can be installed after the doors are mounted and the cabinet is secured in place. If this cabinet is a stand-alone, you should inset the legs 3½" on each side. If the cabinet is in a run of cabinets, you have to inset only the outside units to secure the kick board. Toe kick board clips are attached to the kick board. These metal clips slip on the leg shafts and hold the board securely.

10 Now install your countertop. Either a standard rolled-edge counter top or a custom top can be attached. The screws can be hidden with a number of screw cover caps such as the white ones shown here.

TIP *To properly secure plastic screw head caps and ensure they'll stay in place, do not drive the screw lower than the surface of the board.*

PERFECT DOOR PLACEMENT

It's easy to guarantee perfect door placement using this simple installation method. First, cut a ³⁄₁₆" thick spacer. Then, place the door in its correct open position making sure the vertical alignment is correct. The spacer strip is placed between the door and cabinet side edge. Insert screws through the hinge plate and into the cabinet side board. After both hinges are secure, remove the door from the hinge plates and install the screws in the plate that are hidden by the hinge. Reinstall the doors and adjust if necessary.

Notice that I've placed a block under the cabinet. The cabinet bottom and door rest on this block so the door will be held flush with the lower side of the bottom board while I attach the door.

Veneering a Utility Cabinet

Hundreds of veneers are available, everything from the simple preglued white edge tape to large sheets of real wood. Applying wood veneer to the front edges and exposed sides of a cabinet will give it the appearance of a wood cabinet once matching doors are installed. The doors can be wood or veneer-covered particleboard.

When a cabinet side is exposed, wood veneer must be applied. Details on how to apply the veneer sheets are shown in chapter five. The following steps show how to handle the other surfaces.

1 Prior to assembling the cabinet as previously detailed, apply wood edge tape to the front edges of the side and bottom boards. Then use a router with a flush trim bit to cleanly cut the wood veneer. Drill the shelf pin holes in the cabinet side boards, and attach the side boards to the bottom board using 2" PB screws.

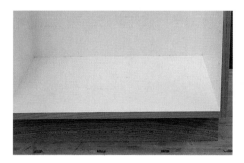

3 Install the cabinet legs and attach leg clips to a veneer PB or solid wood kick board, as the front face will be visible as shown here.

2 Install the back panel with 2" screws at 6" centers. Then attach a solid wood or veneer-covered PB rail with 2" screws.

ADDING A DRAWER

If you plan to add a drawer to a base cabinet, an additional rail is required, as shown here. The amount of drawer height is dependent on the rail position. I always add 1" to my drawer height when determining the lower rail position. For example, if I need a 5" high drawer, I would install the lower rail 6" below the upper rail. In the case of veneered cabinets, the rail is solid wood or veneer-faced PB.

It's also necessary to adjust the door height when adding a drawer. Using a standard utility cabinet with 31" sides as an example, I would need a 22½" high door and a 7" high drawer face. The space between the doors and drawer face is ½" in the center of the bottom rail.

Notice that adding the door height to the

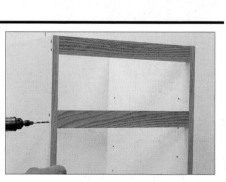

drawer face height, plus the space, equals a total of 30". That's an important dimension when you have a full-door cabinet beside a drawer over door cabinet. The door bottoms are at the same height on each cabinet, and the top edge of the drawer is in line with the top edge of the door on the full-door cabinet. That visual alignment is necessary when a number of cabinets are installed side by side.

TIP *Trimming some veneers, such as oak, can be tricky because the trimmer tends to follow the grain and rip the tape. To solve this problem, use a router with a flush trim bit and lightly sand the edge. Other woods like maple and birch don't have the open grain pattern and are easier to trim. Nevertheless, always use a flush trim bit with wood veneers for a nice clean edge.*

Making a Pot Drawer for a Base Cabinet

A pullout drawer hidden behind a cabinet door is a great way to increase the usefulness of any base cabinet. The drawer glide hardware is often mounted on ¾" thick cleats mounted on the cabinet side so that the drawer will clear the cabinet door.

I'm using ⅝" melamine-coated particleboard for my pull-out drawers. The cabinet's wall-to-wall interior width is 30 ¼". It will be necessary to account for the cleat thickness and the space required for drawer-glide hardware. I'm using Blum 22" bottom mounted drawer glides for this project.

Materials List • Pullout Pot Drawer

REF.	QTY.	PART	STOCK	THICK	WIDTH	LENGTH	COMMENTS
	2	Sides	PB	⅝	7⅜	22	
	2	Front & Back	PB	⅝	7⅜	26½	
	1	Bottom	PB	⅝	27¾	22	
	2	Mounting Cleats	PB	¾	1½	22	

Hardware & Supplies

1 set	22" Bottom Mounted Drawer Glides
	⅝" Cap Molding
	1¼" and 2" PB Screws
	Plastic Screw Cover Caps
	Construction Adhesive
	Matching Edge Tape

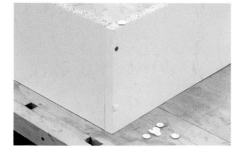

1 Cut the drawer parts. My cabinet width is 30¼", so my drawer width is 30¼" less the cleat thickness and the ½" space per side required for the hardware, or 27¾" wide by 22" deep. The drawer will be 8" high.

2 Use iron-on edge tape and cover the front ends of the drawer sides as well as the side and front edge of the bottom board.

3 Secure the drawer sides to the back and front boards with 2" PB screws.

4 The exposed screw heads should be driven flush with the melamine surface and covered with plastic screw cover caps.

5 Attach the bottom board with 2" PB screws about 6" apart. If the back has been cut accurately, the drawer box will be square.

TIP *You're not limited to a melamine drawer box for pullouts. There are many material options, such as veneer plywood with wood rails, as well as melamine PB with commercial plastic rails.*

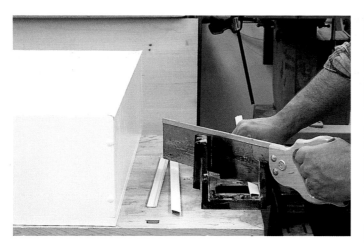

7 Attach the drawer glides according to the manufacturer's instructions.

6 A plastic product called ⅝" cap molding readily available in home stores is cut at 45°angles and is used to cover the drawer edges. The cap molding grips tightly but for maximum hold I always use a little construction adhesive that's available in a caulk tube.

ADDING PULLOUTS IN A CENTER-STILE CABINET

If you want to install pullouts in place of shelves in an older-style base cabinet that has a center stile, first cut the center stile as close to the top and bottom rail as possible. Build and install the pullouts as previously detailed. Then add a board behind one of the doors that will cover the gap previously filled by the center stile.

There will be some damage on the upper and lower rail where the center stile was attached, but it can be sanded smooth and covered with wood veneer edge tape and finished to match the cabinet.

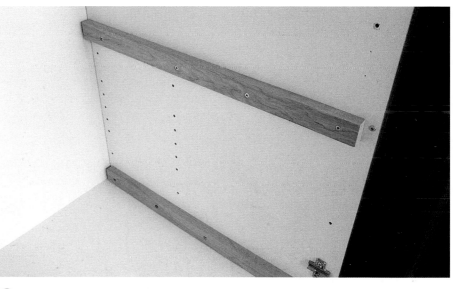

8 Attach the wood cleats to the cabinet walls using 1¼" screws. These cleats must be level and parallel with each other. Space them at least 9" apart so there will be 1" clearance between doors. Notice that I've set my cleats back from the cabinet edge by 1" to leave room for a handle mounted on the front board of the drawer.

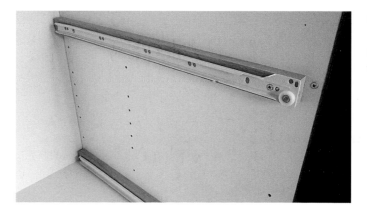

9 Attach the cabinet drawer-glide runners and test fit the drawers.

CHAPTER 5

Utility Wall Cabinets

Utility wall cabinets can be used for many applications, from the laundry room to the garage, in your workshop, or even in the basement. They help you to organize and recover valuable unused space. And best of all, they're simple and inexpensive to build.

A wall cabinet can be made entirely from ⅝" melamine particleboard (PB). A 4' x 8' sheet is about $30 and will provide enough material for two cabinets, including the doors.

To match the decor of any room, wood veneer can be applied to the exterior surfaces of the melamine PB cabinet. A simple flat-panel door can be made from veneer sheet goods, or you can make a more traditional cope-and-stick panel door, as shown here. I'll describe how to build a frameless melamine PB cabinet with a door made from the same material first. Then, I'll explain how to veneer the exterior surfaces when a more formal-looking cabinet is needed.

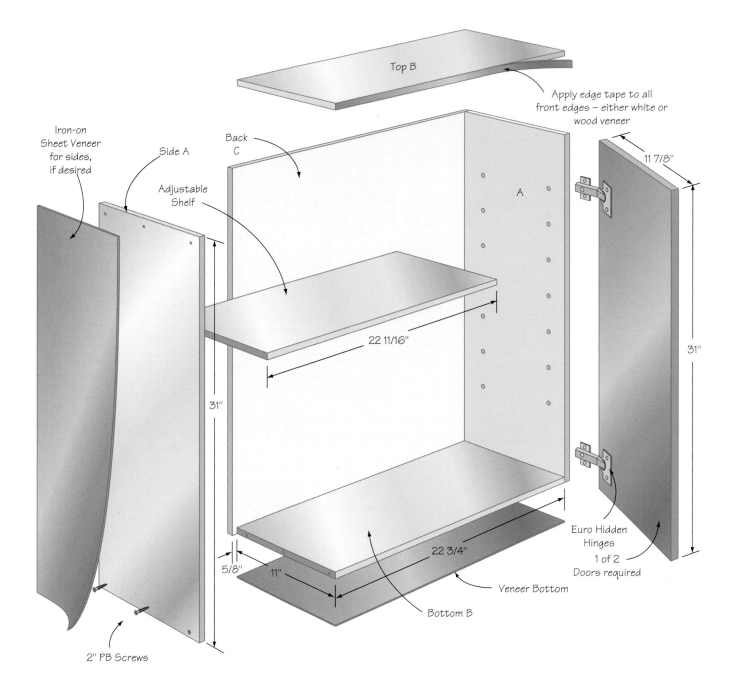

Top B

Apply edge tape to all
front edges – either white or
wood veneer

Iron-on
Sheet Veneer
for sides,
if desired

Side A

Back
C

Adjustable
Shelf

11 7/8"

A

22 11/16"

31"

31"

5/8"

11"

22 3/4"

Euro Hidden
Hinges

1 of 2
Doors required

Veneer Bottom

Bottom B

2" PB Screws

Materials List • Utility Wall Cabinets

REF.	QTY.	PART	STOCK	THICK	WIDTH	LENGTH	COMMENTS
A	2	Side	PB	⅝	11	31	
B	2	Top and Bottom	PB	⅝	11	22¾	
C	1	Back	PB	⅝	24	31	
	2	Doors	PB	⅝	11⅞	31	
	1	Shelf	PB	⅝	11	22¹¹⁄₁₆	

Hardware & Supplies

	2" and 3" PB Screws		⅝" Plastic Cap Molding
4	Hidden Hinges		Construction Ashesive
2	Door Handles		Iron-on Sheet Veneer (if desired)
4	Shelf Pins		Iron-on Edge Tape (either white or veneer)

Calculating Cabinet Width

CABINET WIDTH	TWO SIDES D × H	ONE BOTTOM D × W	ONE BACK W × H
12"	11" × 31"	11" × 10¾"	12" × 31"
15"	11" × 31"	11" × 13¾"	15" × 31"
18"	11" × 31"	11" × 16¾"	18" × 31"
21"	11" × 31"	11" × 19¾"	21" × 31"
24"	11" × 31"	11" × 22¾"	24" × 31"
27"	11" × 31"	11" × 25¾"	27" × 31"
30"	11" × 31"	11" × 28¾"	30" × 31"
33"	11" × 31"	11" × 31¾"	33" × 31"
36"	11" × 31"	11" × 34¾"	36" × 31"

CALCULATING FRAMELESS WALL CABINET DOOR SIZE

Frameless cabinet door heights are the same as the cabinet side board height. The width, when you are going to install the door(s) using full-overlay hidden hinges, is found by measuring the bottom and adding 1" to that dimension. A 12" wide cabinet will require an 11¾"-wide by 31"-high door.

When calculating doors for wider cabinets, add an inch to the bottom width and divide by 2. I wouldn't recommend using a single door when the cabinet is greater than 18" wide.

A 24" wide wall cabinet will need two 11⅞" wide by 31" high doors using the same formula.

REQUIRED TOOLS

Table or circular saw

Jigsaw or band saw

T-square jig

Combination square

Hammer

Nail set

Drill

Screwdrivers

Iron

Building the Basic Wall Cabinet

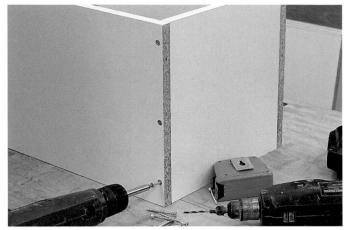

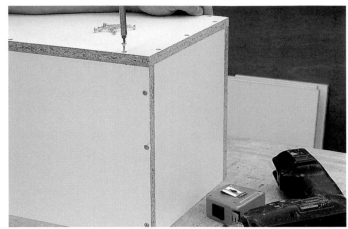

1 After cutting all the cabinet parts to size and applying edge tape as needed, drill holes for the shelf pins. Then attach the sides A to the top and bottom boards B using 2" PB screws at 6" centers. Be certain to drill a pilot hole before installing the screws.

2 Install the back C using 2" PB screws in piloted holes. The back, when flush with all outside edges, will square the cabinet.

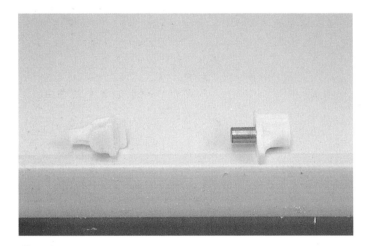

3 Cut the shelf board to size (it is normally as deep as the bottom board and 1/16" narrower), and with construction adhesive, glue on 5/8" plastic cap molding over the front edge of the shelf. This tight-fitting molding is available at all building centers. As with the base cabinet, I'm using 5/16" plastic and steel shelf pins to support the shelf.

4 Cut the door to size using the formula discussed earlier and install the door. All that's left to do is to hang the cabinet to the wall studs using 3" wood screws through the back.

Veneering the Wall Cabinet

Veneered wall cabinets are built in the same way as a melamine utility wall cabinet. However, the exposed edges of the cabinet are covered with wood edge tape, and any exposed side, as well as the cabinet bottom, must be covered with sheet veneer. The door can be a traditional wood door or a flat-panel door made of wood veneer PB.

CALCULATING NON-STANDARD SIZE CABINETS

When you need a cabinet of a specific size, calculate the part sizes based on the cabinet width you require. As an example, let's say I want to build a a cabinet over my clothes dryer, and I need the cabinet to be 23¾" wide by 18" deep. I also know that I'll be using ⅝" thick melamine PB as my building material.

Based on this example, my cabinet side boards would be 18"-deep by 31"-high. The top and bottom boards will be equal to the total cabinet width minus the 2 side board thicknesses, or 18"-deep by 22½"-wide. My back is 23¾"-wide by 31"-high. Using the door calculation formula for full-overlay hidden hinges, I will need two doors that each measure 11¾"-wide by 31"-high.

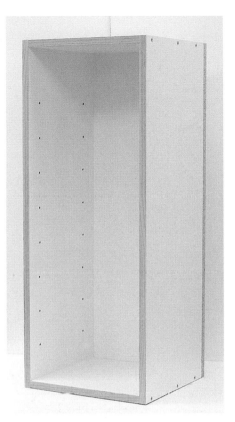

1 After building the cabinet as described in the previous steps, cover the exposed edges with wood edge tape.

TIP *There are two main types of sheet wood veneer: iron-on preglued sheets and nonglued material that must be installed using contact cement. Sheets come in many sizes up to 24" x 96" and are available at many lumber supply stores. Before applying the veneer, be sure to fill any dents or screw holes, or sand smooth any bumps in your surface, as these irregularities will be visible after the veneer is applied.*

2 Apply sheet wood veneer to any exposed cabinet surface. In this application, both the sides and the bottom are visible, so they will all be covered.

CHAPTER 6

Awards Display Case

Children accomplish many things as they grow and are often recognized for those achievements. Awards, plaques, trophies and certificates can be found in most bedrooms.

Often they collect "treasures" like stuffed animals, model cars, or dolls. But there's never enough room to display these precious items. Well, here's a great-looking case that's simple to build for displaying all those treasures. It's made of standard 1×8 solid knotty pine, but any wood can be used. The doors are raised-panel tongue and groove made on a table saw. However, If you don't have a saw, you can buy ready-made doors or use glued-up panels from the home store.

I've used hidden hinges to mount the doors. If you don't own a drill press and a 35mm-hinge boring bit, many other styles of hinges can be used.

I've used the most basic joint and fastener to complete this project—the butt joint with screws and glue. Counterbore the screw holes and fill them with wood plugs. It's a strong joint that looks great and is easy to do. But if you are more experienced and feel comfortable with advanced joinery procedures, you can use biscuits, dowels or dado joints.

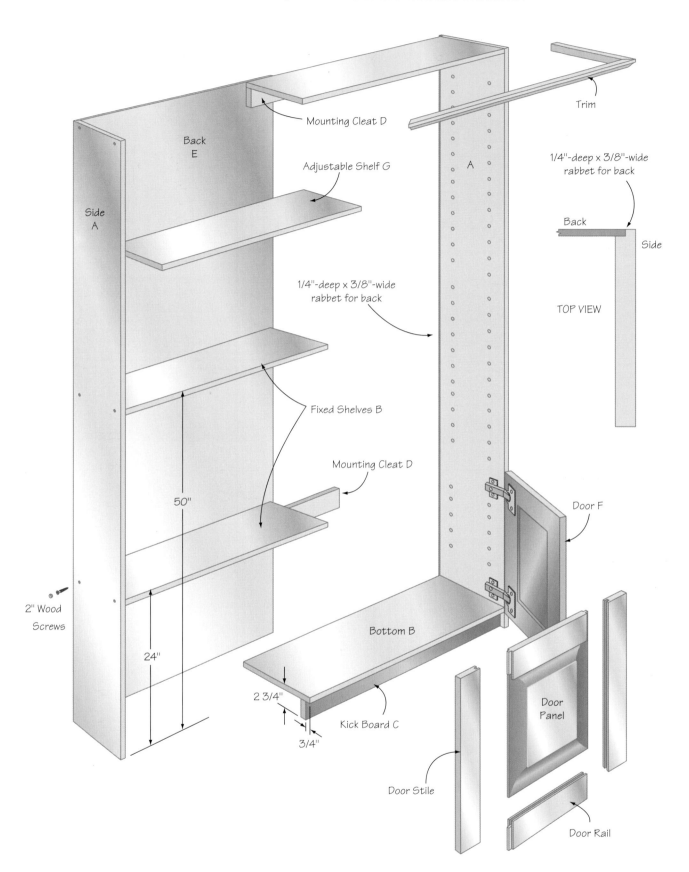

Mounting Cleat D

Trim

Back
E

Adjustable Shelf G

1/4"-deep x 3/8"-wide
rabbet for back

A

Side
A

Back

Side

1/4"-deep x 3/8"-wide
rabbet for back

TOP VIEW

Fixed Shelves B

Mounting Cleat D

Door F

50"

2" Wood
Screws

24"

Bottom B

2 3/4"

Kick Board C

3/4"

Door
Panel

Door Stile

Door Rail

Materials List • Awards Display Case

REF.	QTY.	PART	STOCK	THICK	WIDTH	LENGTH	COMMENTS
A	2	Sides	Pine	¾	7¼	84	
B	4	Fixed Shelves	Pine	¾	7	34½	
C	1	Kick Board	Pine	¾	2	34½	
D	2	Mounting Cleats	Pine	¾	2	34½	
E	1	Back	Pine	¼	35¼	82	
F	2	Doors	Pine	¾	17¾	21½	See "Building Frame and Raised Panel Doors on a Table Saw"
G	6	Adjustable Shelves	Pine	¾	6¾	34⅝	

Hardware and Supplies

	2" Wood Screws	
	Wood Plugs	
	1" Finishing Nails	
24	Shelf Pins	
4	Hidden Hinges	
2	Door Pulls	
5'	Molding	
	Carpenter's Glue	

REQUIRED TOOLS

Table or circular saw

Jigsaw or band saw

T-square jig

Combination square

Hammer

Nail set

Drill

Router

Screwdrivers

Building the Case

The plans for this case can be altered to suit your specific needs. Make it deeper using 1 × 12 stock, build it higher or wider, use premade doors or no doors at all: the options are endless.

1 Cut the sides A as detailed in the materials list. Then cut a ¼"-deep by ⅜"-wide rabbet on the back inside edge of both sides.

2 Attach one fixed shelf B flush at the top, one 2¾" from the bottom, the third at 24" from the bottom, and the fourth at 50" from the bottom. Use 2" wood screws in counterbored holes filled with a wood plug as shown here.

3 Install the kick board C under the bottom shelf. Set it back ¾" from the front edge of the case. Use glue and 2" wood screws through each side board.

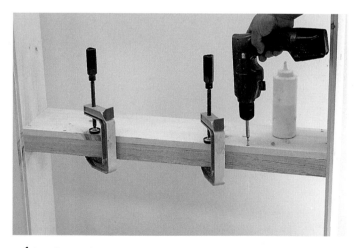

4 Install two cleats D to serve as wall anchors: one under the 24" high shelf and the other under the top shelf. Install screws from the sides and through the fixed shelves.

TIP *If you don't have the equipment to rabbet the sides, attach a 36"-wide back with nails and glue to the back edges of the sides instead. Also, leave the fixed shelves at 7¼" rather than at 7" deep if you won't be using the rabbet.*

Using Dowels

Dowel joinery is another popular method used to join boards. Prior to the biscuit joint, it was commonly used in furniture shops. Alignment is critical with dowel joinery, so most woodworkers use dowel centers to align the holes, as shown here.

6 Round over all the front edges of the case, but leave the top fixed shelf straight so the molding will sit flat. Use a ¼" round over bit in a router or ease the edges by hand with sandpaper as shown here.

5 Attach the back E with glue and 1" finishing nails. The 34½" wide back will fit into the side board rabbets. If you choose not to cut the rabbets, make the back 36" wide.

7 Attach the molding to the top with glue and finishing nails. Countersink the nail heads and fill the holes. The molding style isn't critical, so choose one that suits your taste. Install it flush with the bottom edge of the top fixed shelf.

8 With a shelf-hole jig to ensure accuracy, drill as many pin holes as needed to allow plenty of versatility for your unit.

Building Frame & Raised-Panel Doors on a Table Saw

If you plan to install doors on the lower section, you'll need two doors 17¾"-wide by 21½"-high. They are attached with hidden hinges and are aligned flush with the lower edge of the bottom fixed shelf. The doors can be made from flat glued-up panels that are available at the local lumber store. Or you can make elegant raised-panel doors on a table saw.

Materials List • Raised-Panel Doors

REF.	QTY.	PART	STOCK	THICK	WIDTH	LENGTH	COMMENTS
	4	Stiles	Pine	¾	2¼	21½	
	4	Rails	Pine	¾	2¼	14¼	
	2	Panels	Pine	¾	14⅛	17⅛	Glued-up finished cut dimensions

Hardware and Supplies

Carpenter's Glue and Foam Strips

1 After cutting the stiles and rails to size, use the table saw and make a groove ¼"-wide by ½"-deep on one edge of each rail and stile. Center the groove on each edge.

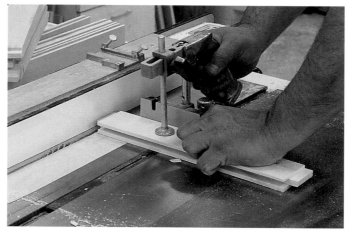

2 With the table saw, cut ¼"-thick by ½"-long tenons centered on each end of both rails. Make the shoulder cut first and then nibble the waste material towards the end of each rail.

TIP *A solid ¾" panel is required for each door. If you have an accurately tuned table saw and a biscuit joiner, you can make your own edge-glued panels. Likewise, you can make them without biscuits by simply edge-gluing boards. Or you can purchase glued panels at most local home stores or lumberyards.*

3 After gluing up and cutting your panels to size, score each panel with the table saw ⅛"-deep and 2" in from each edge.

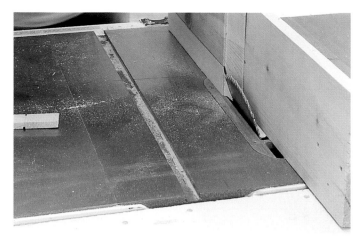

4 Raise the panel by cutting a 10° taper, with the resulting outside edge thickness of ³⁄₁₆".

5 Sand the raised section of your panel with a large flat sanding block. Assemble the door using glue on the tenon only; do not glue the panel. Place small strips of foam in the grooves before inserting the panel to keep the door from rattling.

6 Drill two 35mm holes in each door and install the hidden hinges. (Refer to chapter one for mounting instructions.)

HINGE AND PANEL OPTIONS

Hidden hinges require a 35mm hole. But if you don't have a drill press, other hinges can be used. Many types are available that operate much like the hidden hinge but which are surface mounted. Purchase the hinges before you make the doors.

The stiles and rails can be prepared as previously described, and a ¼" thick veneer-covered plywood panel can be used in place of the solid raised-panel door. This is called a frame-and-flat-panel door. It's a low-cost option and it looks great.

PANEL-TO-FRAME RELATIONSHIP

Flat-panel doors have ¼" thick plywood center panels so they are always lower than the surface of the frame. Raised-panel doors use solid wood panels that have their edges milled. The panel face can be lower or on the same plane as the frame facing. You can control the panel position by deciding upon the frame and panel thickness before starting to build a door.

To make a door with the raised-panel top surface on the same level as the frame members use ¾"-thick frame boards with a ⁹⁄₁₆"-thick panel that fits in a groove cut ³⁄₁₆" in from the back face of the frame members. Or you can use a combination of ⅛"-thick frame pieces with a ⅝"-panel set ¼" in from the back face of the frame members.

If you want the panel face raised above the frame-member front faces, use the same thickness frame and panel pieces. It's a style choice that you can decide upon after making a few sample doors.

CHAPTER 7

Freestanding Pantry

Many kitchens have a storage problem. There's never enough space for all the canned goods, packaged foods and bulk items like flour and sugar. We cram all these goods into every corner of our kitchens and finding them is sometimes quite a challenge.

Here's a project that just might solve your kitchen storage problem. It measures 3'-wide by 2'-deep, but this small cabinet can easily store two weeks of groceries.

I've made this cabinet with pine veneer medium density fiberboard (MDF). The raised-panel stile-and-rail doors are made of solid pine, and can be either purchased or built.

The heart of this pantry is the pullout shelf system. I've used an adjustable version manufactured by Vogt Industries. However, you can make your own pullouts like those detailed in chapter four. If you want a simple and inexpensive version, you could even install adjustable shelves.

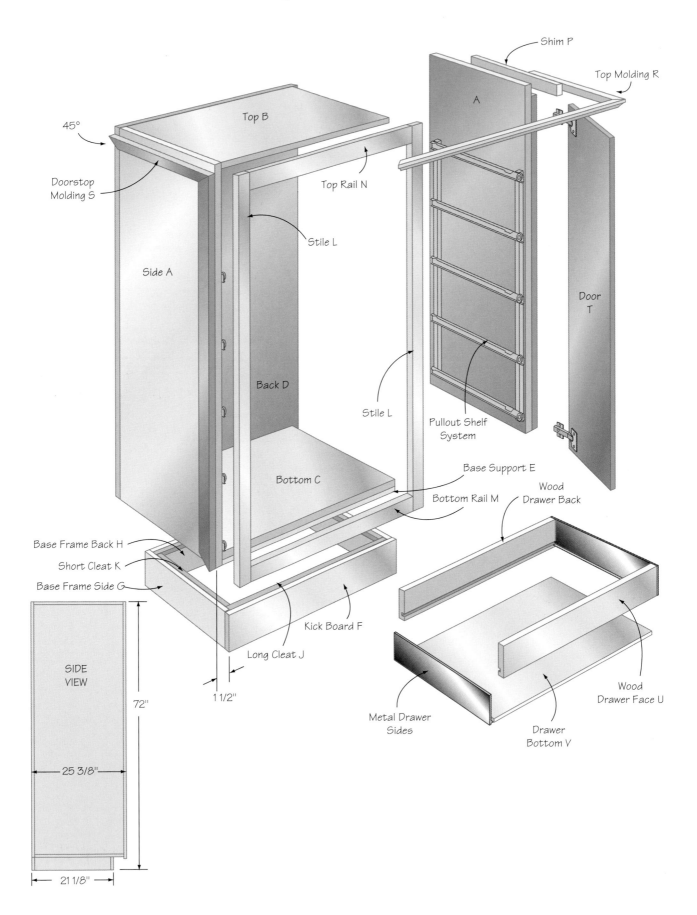

Shim P

Top Molding R

A

45°

Top B

Doorstop Molding S

Top Rail N

Stile L

Side A

Door T

Back D

Stile L

Pullout Shelf System

Bottom C

Base Support E

Bottom Rail M

Wood Drawer Back

Base Frame Back H

Short Cleat K

Base Frame Side G

Kick Board F

Long Cleat J

SIDE VIEW

72"

1 1/2"

25 3/8"

21 1/8"

Metal Drawer Sides

Drawer Bottom V

Wood Drawer Face U

Materials List • Freestanding Pantry

REF.	QTY.	PART	STOCK	THICK	WIDTH	LENGTH	COMMENTS
A	2	Sides	MDF	¾	23⅞	68	
B	1	Top	MDF	¾	23⅞	34½	
C	1	Bottom	MDF	¾	23⅞	34½	
D	1	Back	MDF	¾	36	68	
E	1	Base Support	MDF	½	24⅝	36	
F	1	Kick Board	Pine	¾	3½	33	
G	2	Base Sides	Pine	¾	3½	20⅜	
H	1	Base Frame back	Pine	¾	3½	31½	
J	2	Base Cleats	Pine	¾	¾	31½	
K	2	Base Cleats	Pine	¾	¾	18	
L	2	Stiles	Pine	¾	1	68½	
M	1	Bottom Rail	Pine	¾	1¼	34½	
N	1	Top Rail	Pine	¾	1½	34½	
P	2	Molding Shims	Pine	¾	1⅛	24⅝	
T	2	Doors	Pine	¾	17¾	67¼	
U	10	Drawer fronts & backs	Pine	¾	—	—	Determine width and height according to
V	5	Drawer Bottoms	MDF	½	—	—	the manufacturer's instructions if you use
	(½" Drawer Bottoms recommended for extra support of heavy canned goods.)						pullout system with drawer sides provided
R	8'	Top molding	Pine				
S	40'	Door Stop Molding	Pine				

Hardware and Supplies

		⅜" Wood Plugs
		Carpenter's Glue
		Material for Pullouts or Fixed Shelves as Required
		2" Finish Nails and 1" Brad Nails
		1", 1½" and 2" PB Screws
		Wood Putty
	6	Hidden Hinges
	2	Door Pulls

REQUIRED TOOLS

- Table or circular saw
- Jigsaw or band saw
- T-square jig
- Combination square
- Hammer
- Nail set
- Drill
- Screwdrivers

Building the Pantry

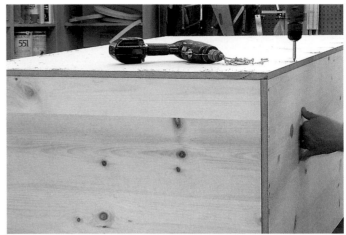

1 Cut the two cabinet sides A, top B and bottom C as detailed in the materials list. Join the sides to the top and bottom boards using glue and 2" PB screws. Remember to predrill prior to installing the screws for the maximum hold. The cabinet box should measure 36"-wide by 68"-high.

2 Attach the back with glue and 2" PB screws in predrilled holes. An accurately cut back will square the cabinet box.

3 Since this cabinet will carry a great deal of weight, reinforce the bottom using a piece of ½"-thick plywood that measures 24⅝"-deep by 36"-wide. Glue and screw it in place using 1" screws.

4 Mark a line on the bottom of the base 3½" in from the cabinet front and 1½" in from each side to indicate the placement of the base frame. Then construct a 3½"-high base frame F, G and H using ¾" solid stock, and measuring 21⅝"-deep by 33"-wide. Assemble the frame with glue and 2" screws in counterbored holes, and fill the holes with wood plugs.

5 Cut the four cleats J and K as detailed in the materials list, and attach them with glue and screws to the inside top edge of the base frame. Then apply glue to the top edge of the base frame and place the assembly on the base using the guide marks. Screw through the cleats into the base with 1½" screws.

6 Attach the stiles L with glue and 2" finishing nails. Be sure the stile inside face is flush with the side inside face. Set the nail heads and fill the holes with colored wood putty.

7 Attach the bottom rail M in the same manner so that its bottom edge is aligned to the ends of each stile.

8 Attach the top rail N so that its top edge is flush with the stile ends.

9 Glue and nail both molding shims P to both top edges of the cabinet. These strips will allow easy installation of crown molding.

10 Choose a top molding R to suit your decor. I am using 1 ⅛" high molding, but any size or style is fine. If the molding is higher than 1 ⅛", install it above the cabinet top. Do not attach molding lower than 1 ⅛" below the top edge as we will need clearance for door overlap.

11 Once the crown is attached, install doorstop molding S around the perimeter of each side. Use glue and brad nails. Miter each corner with the round edge of the molding facing inward.

12 Install your slide and support assemblies. There are many shelving options. I am using a system of adjustable pullouts that can be purchased at most kitchen hardware supply stores.

Any number of door styles can be used on the pantry cabinet. You'll need two doors, each 17¾"-wide by 67¼"-high. I would suggest that you use three full-overlay hidden hinges per door because of the door size. Using these types of hinges makes door-width calculation easier.

There are many door suppliers, so it's a simple matter to order two doors for the cabinet. But if you prefer, you can build raised-panel doors on the table saw as detailed in the previous chapter.

I prefer to cover the bottom rail with a door and overlap the top rail by ¼". The distance from the bottom rail to the inside edge of the top rail is 67". Add ¼" for overlap, and the door height will be 67 ¼". That's a standard method for calculating door heights for cabinets with full-overlay doors.

The width of any cabinet door or pair of doors is also easily calculated. Measure the inside opening of the cabinet. In this case, it's 34½". If you have stiles extending into the cabinet, measure their inside dimension. But in this case the inside edge of the stiles is mounted flush with the interior face of the cabinet sides. Add 1" to that dimension for a total measurement of 35½".

Therefore, the cabinet requires two 17¾"-wide doors that are 67¼"-high.

TIP *Veneer MDF or particleboard material readily accepts a stain, so your final color can be custom matched to any cabinet.*

For my pantry, I finished it with three coats of oil-based polyurethane. I cut the first coat by 10 percent with thinner and sanded with 320-grit paper between coats.

13 All that's left to make are the drawer fronts, backs and bottoms. The wood for the fronts normally matches the cabinet wood.

CHAPTER 8

Seven-Drawer Chest

Bedrooms never have enough drawer space. Most of us have undergarments, socks, T-shirts and other clothing items that are ideally suited for drawer storage. So, improve the situation in your children's bedroom, or even your own, and build this project.

This high chest has seven relatively shallow drawers. You can make the same project with deeper drawers, but there will not be as many drawers. But no matter what the size, all chests are built in basically the same fashion. Once you've built one like the one in this chapter, you will be able to build a size to suit your specific needs.

Many woodworkers feel a great deal of skill is needed to build a chest or dresser. Nothing could be farther from the truth. It is a simple process. Take your time and perform each step in order. You'll soon see how easy it is to build great-looking bedroom furniture.

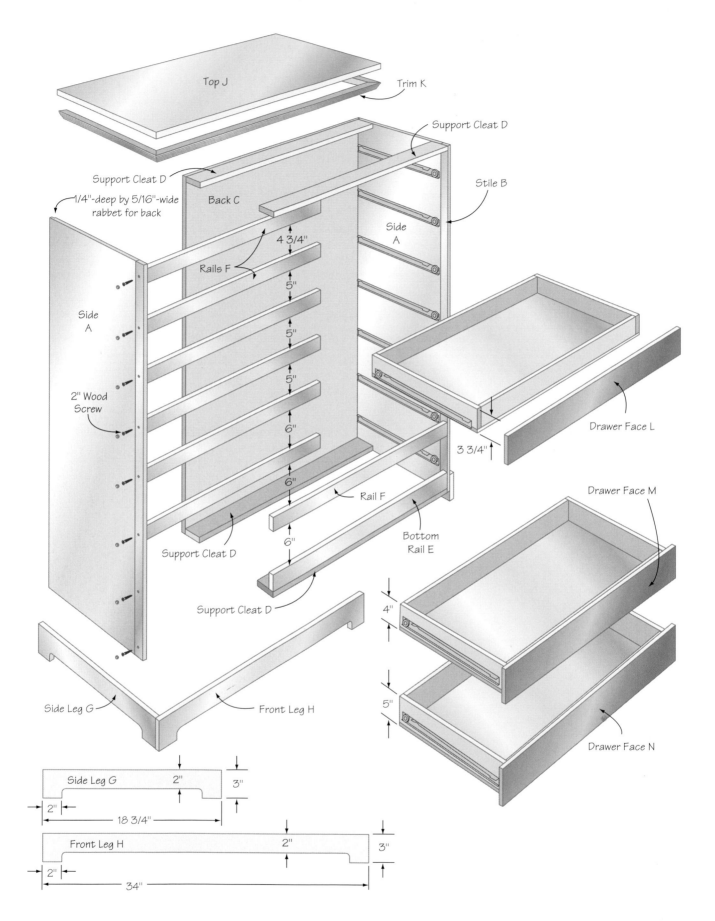

Top J

Trim K

Support Cleat D

Support Cleat D

Stile B

1/4"-deep by 5/16"-wide rabbet for back

Back C

Side A

4 3/4"

Rails F

Side A

5"

5"

5"

2" Wood Screw

6"

Drawer Face L

6"

3 3/4"

Rail F

6"

Drawer Face M

Support Cleat D

Bottom Rail E

Support Cleat D

4"

Side Leg G

Front Leg H

5"

Drawer Face N

Side Leg G   2"   3"

2"

18 3/4"

Front Leg H   2"   3"

2"

34"

Materials List • Seven-Drawer Chest

REF.	QTY.	PART	STOCK	THICK	WIDTH	LENGTH	COMMENTS
A	2	Sides	Veneered PB	¹¹⁄₁₆	18	52	
B	2	Stiles	Hardwood	¹¹⁄₁₆	¾	52	
C	1	Back	Veneered PB	¼	31¾	52	
D	4	Support Cleats	Veneered PB	¾	2½	31⅛	
E	1	Bottom Rail	Hardwood	¾	2¼	31⅛	
F	7	Rails	Hardwood	¾	1½	31⅛	
G	2	Side Legs	Hardwood	¾	3	18¾	
H	1	Front Leg	Hardwood	¾	3	34	
J	1	Top	Hardwood	¾	19½	34½	
K	1	Molding	Hardwood	¾	1	96	
L	1	Drawer Face	Hardwood	¾	5¼	32	
M	3	Drawer Faces	Hardwood	¾	5½	32	
N	3	Drawer Faces	Hardwood	¾	6½	32	

Tall Drawer Boxes

	6	Sides	Baltic Birch	½	3½	18	
	6	Backs & Fronts	Baltic Birch	½	3½	29⅛	
	3	Bottoms	Baltic Birch	½	18	30⅛	

Medium Drawer Boxes

	6	Sides	Baltic Birch	½	4½	18	
	6	Backs & Fronts	Baltic Birch	½	4½	29⅛	
	3	Bottoms	Baltic Birch	½	18	30⅛	

Narrow Drawer Box

	2	Sides	Baltic Birch	½	3¼	18	
	2	Backs & Fronts	Baltic Birch	½	3¼	29⅛	
	1	Bottom	Baltic Birch	½	18	30⅛	

Hardware and Supplies

7	Drawer Pulls	Brad Nails
7 sets	18" Bottom Mounted Drawer Glides (Blum)	⅜" Wood Plugs
	1", 1¼" and 2" Wood Screws	Carpenter's Glue
	2" Finish Nails	Filler

REQUIRED TOOLS

Table or circular saw

Jigsaw or band saw

T-square jig

Combination square

Hammer

Nail set

Drill

Router

Screwdrivers

Building the Carcase

1 Cut the two side panels A to size. Then cut a ¼"-deep by ⁵⁄₁₆"-wide rabbet on the back inside face of both side panels to receive the back. (The rabbet can be cut with a hand held router, a router table or a table saw equipped with a dado blade.)

2 Use glue and 2" finishing nails to secure the stiles B. Countersink the nail heads and fill the holes with colored filler that will match the final finish.

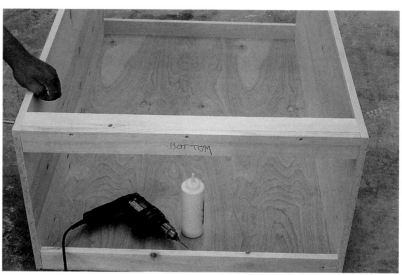

4 Attach the bottom rail E with glue and screws through the side panels and bottom cleat. Use 2" screws in predrilled holes for the maximum holding power.

TIP *Always try to use a screw or nail whose length is twice the thickness of the board you are screwing through. But remember that the screw is there only to provide a good mechanical bond while the glue cures. Once that happens, the glue is the bonding agent. However, you need a solid mechanical bond for the glue to cure properly.*

3 Cut and attach the four support cleats D. Then fit the back into the rabbets and attach it with glue and brad nails through the rear and into each side panel. Since I want my chest carcass to have a finished width of 32½", my back is 31¾" plus the remaining thickness of each side panel after the rabbets have been cut.

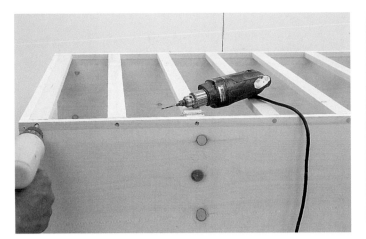

5 Attach the remaining seven rails F with glue and screws through the outside of each stile. Use 2" screws in predrilled counterbored holes so wood plugs can be installed. (One screw per side is adequate.) Make sure the placement of the rails allow for three bottom drawers that are 6" high, three middle drawers that are 5" high and a top drawer that is 4¾" high.

6 Cut out each side leg G, round over the top, bottom and back edges with a ¼" router bit, and install each leg 1½" up from the bottom edge of the side panels. Use glue and four 1¼" screws through the inside of the cabinet side panels.

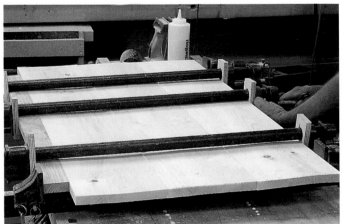

7 Cut out the front leg H, round over all edges of the outside face and attach it with glue and 1¼" screws.

8 Make a solid wood top panel J using three ¾"-thick boards edge-glued together. If you haven't got the equipment to edge-glue, pre-made solid wood panels that can be cut to size are available at most large home centers.

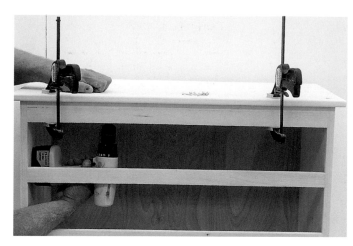

9 Cut the top to a finished size, and round over the top and bottom face of the sides and front with a ¼" roundover bit in a router. Secure the top to the cabinet, making sure it's flush with the back. Use glue and 1¼" screws through the cleats to anchor the top. If you're using a solid wood top, don't use glue. The boards will expand and contract with humidity changes, and the screw-only method will allow a slight bit of room for movement.

10 Install ¾"-thick by 1"-high trim molding K under the chest top. Dozens of styles are available, so choose one that matches the cabinet style.

11 Build the drawers from ½" Baltic birch plywood. Use the sizes detailed in the materials list, and follow the steps outlined in chapter two. To install the bottom-mount drawer glides, first determine the height of the screw line above each rail for your particular brand of drawer glides. (The Blum drawer glides I use are installed by drawing a center screw line on the side panel ¾" above the rail.) Lay the chest carcass on its back and use a carpenter's square to draw a straight line to indicate the center of each screw hole. Install one ⅝" screw in the front and one at the back (in the adjusting screw hole) of each glide. Inset the remaining screws once you test the drawers. If a slight adjustment is necessary, loosen the back screw and align the glide.

12 Check the fit and alignment of each drawer box. If a box doesn't sit properly on the glides, adjust it by slightly raising or lowering one side rail. Once the drawers are correct, install the remaining rail screws.

CONSTRUCTION OPTIONS

This basic construction method can be used when building dressers as well as chests. Dressers tend to have two banks of drawers, which means you'll have to add a center panel and center stile. But no matter what style of chest or dresser you need, build it following the procedures just outlined.

Wood Choices

Many species of wood are available. Some are easier than others to work. The final finish often determines the choice of wood. For example, if I want a painted dresser, I would probably use poplar or ash, as they are relatively inexpensive hardwoods that readily accept paint.

Veneer-covered MDF or particleboard is often the panel of choice when building cabinets. But, if you have a source of wood, and the equipment to glue up solid panels, that's the way to go.

Details and Trim

Details such as the legs and trim can be altered to dramatically change the looks of your project. Thicker legs, tops and trim give the piece a heavy look. Thinner tops and detailed trim lighten the appearance. So experiment with a few scraps of wood to achieve the "look" you desire.

13 Round over the outside edges of the drawer faces L, M and N with a ¼" round over bit. Secure each face to the drawer box using four 1" screws. Since the top drawer face can't be attached by reaching through the next higher drawer box space, drill the hole for the hardware you plan on using, and temporarily attach the drawer face to the box using a 1¼" screw through the hardware hole. The drawer can then be opened with the face securely in place. Once the face is attached from the inside, remove the screw from the front and install the hardware.

CHAPTER 9

Teen's Work Center

We all tend to work better when we are organized. Information and the materials needed to work and study are more effectively used when they are within easy reach. The same situation applies to your children. They will work better when they have a dedicated, organized area for their projects and homework. To answer those needs, I've designed a work center that may help get them better organized.

This project is made of solid pine and composite veneer board. It's reasonably easy to build and not very expensive. If the desk is too small or large for your space, change the dimensions. The only major difference between this desk and a wider unit is the hutch width. If you need a 30" x 60" desktop, add the extra width onto the horizontal members of the hutch. And if you do have the space for a deeper desktop, consider building the hutch with 1 x 12 lumber.

I've used ¾" pine veneer MDF for the large panels. However, particleboard or solid wood panels can be substituted. If you plan on painting the center, use plain MDF as an inexpensive alternative. It's a great product and is easily painted.

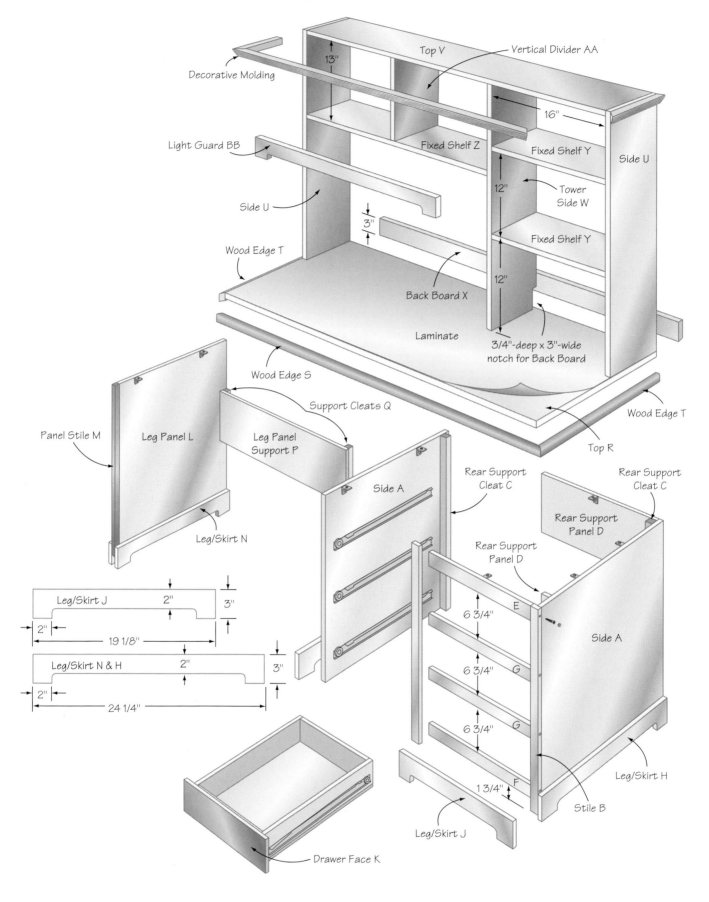

Decorative Molding

13"

Top V

Vertical Divider AA

16"

Light Guard BB

Fixed Shelf Z

Fixed Shelf Y

Side U

Side U

12"

Tower
Side W

3"

Fixed Shelf Y

Wood Edge T

12"

Back Board X

Laminate

3/4"-deep x 3"-wide
notch for Back Board

Wood Edge S

Support Cleats Q

Wood Edge T

Panel Stile M

Leg Panel L

Leg Panel
Support P

Top R

Side A

Rear Support
Cleat C

Rear Support
Cleat C

Rear Support
Panel D

Leg/Skirt N

Rear Support
Panel D

Leg/Skirt J   2"

3"

E

6 3/4"

2"

19 1/8"

Side A

Leg/Skirt N & H   2"

3"

6 3/4"   G

2"

24 1/4"

6 3/4"   G

Leg/Skirt H

1 3/4"   F

Stile B

Leg/Skirt J

Drawer Face K

80

Materials List • Teen's Work Center

REF.	QTY.	PART	STOCK	THICK	WIDTH	LENGTH	COMMENTS
Drawer Bank							
A	2	Sides	Veneered MDF	¾	23½	27½	
B	2	Stiles	Pine	¾	¾	29¼	
C	2	Rear Support cleats	Hardwood	¾	¾	27½	
D	2	Rear Support panels	Veneered MDF	¾	7	16	
E	1	Top Rail	Pine	¾	2¼	16	
F	1	Bottom Rail	Pine	¾	2	16	
G	2	Middle Rails	Pine	¾	1½	16	
H	2	Leg/Skirts	Pine	¾	3	24¼	
J	1	Front Leg	Pine	¾	3	19⅛	
not shown	6	Drawer Sides	Baltic Birch	½	5¼	22	
not shown	6	Drawer Front/Back	Baltic Birch	½	5¼	14	
not shown	3	Drawer Bottoms	Baltic Birch	½	15	22	
K	3	Drawer Faces	Pine	¾	7¼	17	
Leg Panel and Support							
L	1	Leg Panel	Veneered MDF	¾	23½	27½	
M	1	Panel Stile	Pine	¾	¾	29¼	
N	2	Leg/Skirts	Pine	¾	3	24¼	
P	1	Leg Panel Support	Veneered MDF	¾	7¼	29¾	
Q	2	Support Cleats	Hardwood	¾	¾	7¼	
Desktop							
R	1	Desktop	PB	¾	24½	48	
S	1	Front Edge	Pine	¾	1½	49½	
T	2	Side Edges	Pine	¾	1½	24½	
Desk Hutch							
U	2	Sides	Pine	¾	7¼	36	
V	1	Top	Pine	¾	7¼	46½	
W	1	Tower Side	Pine	¾	7¼	35¼	
X	1	Backboard	Pine	¾	3	46½	
Y	2	Fixed Shelves	Pine	¾	7¼	16	
Z	1	Fixed Shelf	Pine	¾	7¼	29¾	
AA	1	Vertical Divider	Pine	¾	7¼	13	
BB	1	Light Guard	Pine	¾	4	29¾	

Hardware & Supplies

1 sheet	28" x 52" High-Pressure Laminate	Wood Plugs
	6'-Decorative Molding	Finish and Brad Nails
3 sets	22" Bottom-Mount Drawer Glides	Colored Wood Filler
3	Drawer Handles	⅝", 1", 1¼" and 2" PB Screws
6	Right-Angle Desktop Brackets	Carpenter's Glue

REQUIRED TOOLS

Table or circular saw

Jigsaw or bandsaw

Drill

Router

Miter box

T-square jig

Combination square

Screwdrivers

Hammer

Nail set

Building the Drawer Bank and Leg Panel Assembly

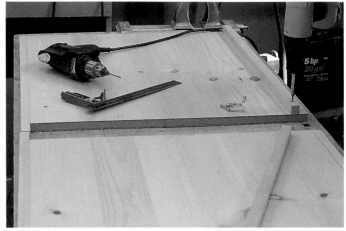

1 Cut the two drawer bank sides A and the leg panel L to size. With glue and finishing nails, attach the stiles B and M to one face of each panel. Attach each stile so it's flush with the top of the panel and extends 1¾" beyond the panel bottom. Countersink the nail heads and fill the holes with colored putty.

2 Cut the two rear support cleats C and, ¾" in from the back edges, secure them to the inside face of each drawer bank side with glue and 1¼" screws. Make sure that you build the two drawer bank sides as mirror images of each other.

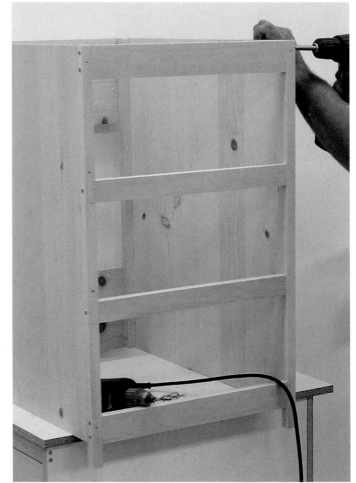

3 Attach the two rear support panels with screws and glue. (Since these two pieces will not be visible, any ¾" material will be fine.)

4 Install the drawer rails E, F and G using glue and 2" screws in pilot holes that have been counterbored to accept wood plugs.

TIP *When cutting multiple patterns such as the leg/skirt assemblies, create a pattern with scrap material to use as a guide. Then, after all the pieces are cut, clamp them together and sand the rough edges. This ensures that all the pieces will be identical.*

5 Cut out the four leg/skirt boards H and N, and round over the top, bottom and back edges of their outsides faces with a ¼" roundover bit. Attach two of the leg/skirt boards H to the drawer bank using 1¼" screws and glue. (The boards are installed flush with the face frame stile and 1¼" up from the bottom edge of the side panels.) Then attach the remaining two legs N to the leg panel in the same manner.

6 Cut out the front skirt J to match the sides, round over all edges of the face side, and attach the board using 1¼" screws and glue. Three screws will hold the board securely until the adhesive cures.

7 Build the drawers from ½" Baltic birch plywood following the steps in chapter two. Then install the 22" bottom-mount drawer glides by first attaching the runners to the drawer box. Use a carpenter's square to draw a screw hole guideline ¾" up from each rail to align the cabinet runners.

8 Make three drawer faces K from 1x8 lumber, round over the edges of the outside faces with a ¼" roundover bit, and attach the drawer faces with 1" screws through the drawer box. Each face should overlap its top and bottom rail by ¼".

9 To complete the drawer bank, install right-angle brackets around the top edge to be used in securing the desktop.

Constructing the Hutch

1 After cutting the pieces for the hutch to size, join the two hutch sides U to the top V using glue and 2" wood screws. The screw heads will be covered by trim molding so they can be driven flush with the side surfaces.

2 Notch the bottom back edge of the tower side panel W to allow for the backboard X. Leave a 16" space for the fixed shelves and secure the tower side through the top in piloted counterbored holes that can be filled with wood plugs,

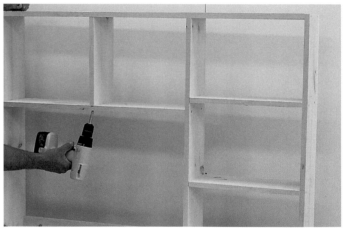

3 Attach the hutch backboard X to the sides U and tower side W using glue and screws through the sides, and install wood plugs. Two screws through the backboard should adequately secure the tower side.

4 Attach the fixed shelves Y and Z, and vertical divider AA with glue and screws. Fill the holes with plugs.

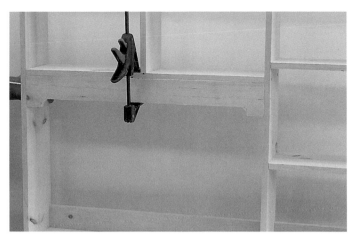

5 If you plan on using a fluorescent fixture beneath the long shelf, cut out and install a light guard BB. Use glue and screws through the sides as well as the top of the long shelf Z.

6 Ease all the front edges of the hutch with the exception of the top board. If you plan on installing 1"-high molding as I've done, stop the roundover procedure at a point where the molding crosses the hutch's vertical boards. This will provide a square flat surface to attach the trim molding.

BUILDING A HIGH-PRESSURE LAMINATE TOP

High-pressure laminates are an excellent choice for the work center top. They provide a smooth writing surface and can take a great deal of abuse. To make this top, I start with a ¾" particleboard or plywood substrate. I attach wood edges to the front and two sides of the board. Then, using contact cement, I glue down a high-pressure laminate to the substrate. Finally, I trim and round over the laminate with my router. (See chapter three for more details on building a desktop.)

For this project, you'll need a panel that's ¾" x 24½" x 48". The front is edged with a ¾" x 1½" x 49½" solid piece of wood. The two side edges are the same height and thickness, but are 24½" long.

The laminate material should be about 28" x 52". That's larger than the actual top, but you'll need a little extra material for easy alignment. The overhang can be cut with a flush trim router bit.

7 Choose a suitable trim molding for the top, and secure it with glue and brad nails. You'll need about 6' of molding and a miter box to cut the 45° corners.

Assembling the Work Center

All of the assembly should be done using only screws. Glue should not be used in case the center needs to be taken apart for moving. And you may need to replace the desktop due to wear or damage.

First, set the desktop on the drawer bank and leg panel. Secure the top to the drawer bank with ⅝" screws in the right-angle brackets. Then, using four 1¼" screws, attach the leg panel to the back side of the wood edge that extends ¾" below the desktop.

Prepare the leg panel support. Verify your exact measurement by making sure the leg panel is plumb, and cut the support board P accordingly. Cut and attach two cleats Q to each end of the support board using glue and 1¼" screws.

Use the leg panel support assembly to join the drawer bank and leg panel. (The support is installed with the cleats on the backside.) Three 1¼" screws will hold the leg panel securely.

Place the hutch on top of the desk. Align the backboard with the back edge of the desktop. Install two screws from the underside of the desktop into the backboard to secure it in place.

Install the drawers and verify all the components fit and operate properly. Finally, take the center apart and apply a finish.

TIP *An effect called* **bridging** *can occur when screwing two boards together. The screw threads into each board and will not draw them tightly to each other.*

To prevent bridging, drill a hole in the board on the screw-head side larger than the thread diameter. The screw will turn freely in that board and draw it tightly to the second board.

CONSTRUCTION OPTIONS

Desks are fun to build because they are useful and appreciated by everyone. And dozens of accessories are available at your local business supply store. You can buy hanging folders for files, pencil trays, storage racks, locks and so on. It's easy to personalize a work center for any member of your family.

Another option would be to use full-extension drawer glides in place of the 3/4 extension bottom-mount hardware. They are more expensive, but almost a necessity when installing a file folder storage system in one of the drawers.

Customizing Sizes

This project is an excellent basic design. But as everyone's needs are different, it's a simple matter to customize the dimensions to make them work for your own personal needs. Sizes can be changed, or drawers can be made deeper if you need a place to store file folders. Hanging-file-folder hardware is very inexpensive and available at any business supply store. If you decide to go that route, buy the hardware first and then build the drawer box to the required size.

The depth and the width of the desktop are easily changed. A 30"-deep desktop will need a deeper leg panel and drawer bank. But you'll gain more storage space from the deeper drawers.

The hutch is a great storage option for any work center. It can be customized with added shelving or adjustable shelves. The depth and height is easily changed to accommodate your needs. Taking the time to design a custom desk hutch is a valuable exercise. Books, reference material, CDs, supplies and all the other necessary items are at your finger tips making the tasks you have to perform much easier.

Other Materials

High-pressure laminates are an excellent choice for the work center that will be heavily used. But you can use wood veneer panels if you want an all wood look. They can be glued up using any size lumber or purchased at your local home center. I've also seen a few desks with wood tops and a glass overlay to protect the wood and to provide a smooth, durable top.

HIDING NAILS AND
SCREW HOLES

Many woodworking operations involve the use of fasteners such as nails and screws. Often they are hidden, but there are times when you must use these fasteners in obvious areas of the project. Attaching face frames to cabinets by using the face-nailing technique is one of the more common situations.

We are fortunate that many manufacturers now make fillers that accept a finish or are colored to match the final finish. One such product is the tinted wood filler paste. With a little practice you can almost make any nail hole invisible. (See photo 1).

Wax sticks are available in many tones that can also be used to fill holes and cracks. These are easily applied by gently heating the wax. (See photo 2).

Screw heads are difficult to fill because of their size. The best solution is to use wood plugs or buttons. (See photo 3).

And finally, as a wise old cabinetmaker told me when I was just starting in this business, "If you can't hide the hole or joint, highlight it." That was a good piece of advice, and I still use it every day.

Tinted wood filler pastes are available to match just about any **finished** wood.

2 Once exclusively sold to professional cabinetmakers and furniture repair technicians, wax and epoxy fillers are now common items in woodworking supply stores.

3 Counterbored pilot holes provide a hole for wood plugs and buttons when a screw hole needs to be concealed.

CHAPTER 10

Platform Storage Bed

The space under our beds collects dust and is a good hiding place for the cat—but that's about the extent of its usefulness. Platform beds make use of that space by providing storage drawers for clothing and bed linens. After building one of these beds, you may have extra room in your dresser drawers or hall closet, and what a nice change that would be.

The platform bed in this chapter is designed for a twin mattress measuring 38" x 74½". But it can be built to accommodate any size mattress from twin to king. Again, as in other chapters, the construction principles remain. Only a few dimensions need changing.

Since my bed project will be against a wall, drawers will be accessible only on the open side. But I've made a mirror-image frame so the drawers can be changed to the opposite side should the need arise. I'm also using bottom-mounted drawer glides, which eliminates a lot of extra framing.

This is a good project to make use of those scrap sheets hanging around your shop. Since much of the support framing will not be visible, just about any ⅝"-to-¾"-thick sheet material will work fine.

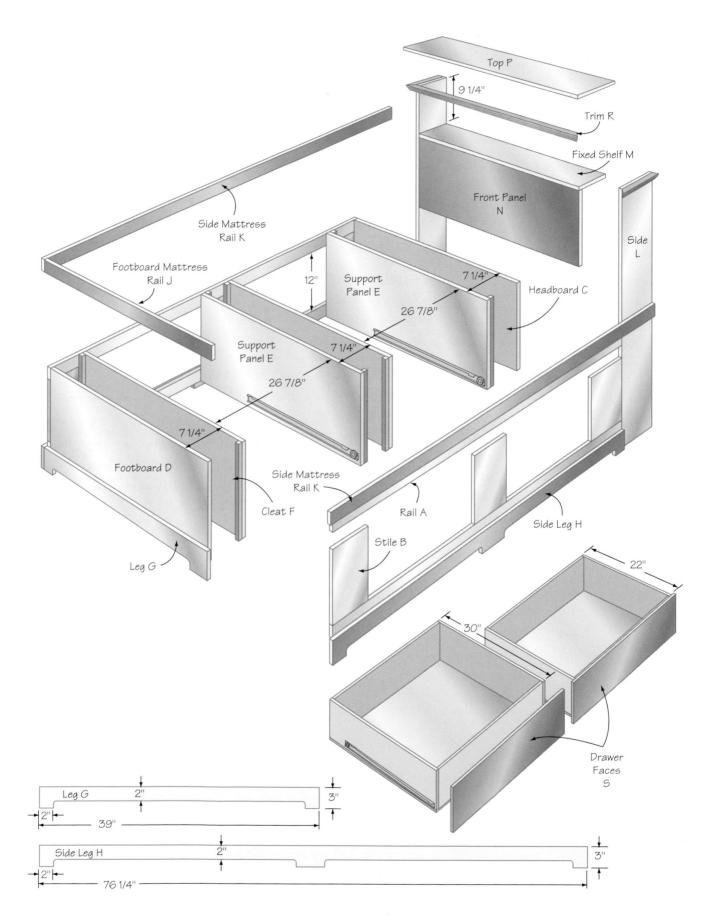

Top P

9 1/4"

Trim R

Fixed Shelf M

Front Panel N

Side L

Side Mattress Rail K

Footboard Mattress Rail J

12"

Support Panel E

7 1/4"

26 7/8"

Headboard C

Support Panel E

7 1/4"

26 7/8"

Footboard D

7 1/4"

Side Mattress Rail K

Cleat F

Rail A

Side Leg H

Stile B

Leg G

22"

30"

Drawer Faces S

Leg G   2"   3"

2"   39"

Side Leg H   2"   3"

2"   76 1/4"

Materials List • Platform Storage Bed

REF.	QTY.	PART	STOCK	THICK	WIDTH	LENGTH	COMMENTS
A	4	Frame Rails	Hardwood	¾	1½	75½	
B	6	Frame Stiles	Hardwood	¾	7¼	12	
C	1	Headboard	Veneer PB	¹¹⁄₁₆	15	37½	
D	1	Footboard	Veneer PB	¹¹⁄₁₆	15	37½	
E	4	Support Panels	PB	⅝	15	37½	
F	8	Mounting Cleats	Hardwood	¾	¾	15	
G	1	Footboard Leg	Hardwood	¾	3	39	
H	2	Side Legs	Hardwood	¾	3	76¼	
J	1	Footboard Mattress Rail	Hardwood	¾	3	39	
K	2	Side Mattress Rails	Hardwood	¾	3	82¼	
L	2	Bookcase Sides	Hardwood	¾	6	38	
M	1	Fixed Shelf	Hardwood	¾	6	37½	
N	1	Front Panel	PB	¹¹⁄₁₆	12	37½	
P	1	Bookcase Top	Hardwood	¾	7¼	41½	
Q	1	Trim Support	Hardwood	¾	1	37½	
R	6'	Trim	Hardwood				
S	2	Drawer Faces	Veneer PB	¾	12½	28	
	1	Mattress Platform	Plywood	¾	39	75½	Not needed if you use a box spring

Drawer Boxes

	QTY.	PART	STOCK	THICK	WIDTH	LENGTH	
	2	Sides	Baltic Birch	½	10½	30	
	2	Backs and Fronts	Baltic Birch	½	10½	24⅞	
	1	Bottom	Baltic Birch	½	25⅞	30	
	2	Sides	Baltic Birch	½	10½	22	
	2	Backs and Fronts	Baltic Birch	½	10½	24⅞	
	1	Bottom	Baltic Birch	½	25⅞	22	

Hardware & Supplies

1 set	30" Bottom Mount Drawer Glides		1¼" and 2" PB Screws	
1 set	22" Bottom Mount Drawer Glides		Finishing and Brad Nails	
2	Drawer Pulls		Carpenter's Glue	
	Matching Edge Tape		Wood Plugs	

REQUIRED TOOLS

Table or circular saw

Jigsaw or band saw

T-square jig

Combination square

Hammer

Nail set

Drill

Router

Screwdrivers

Iron

Constructing the Frame

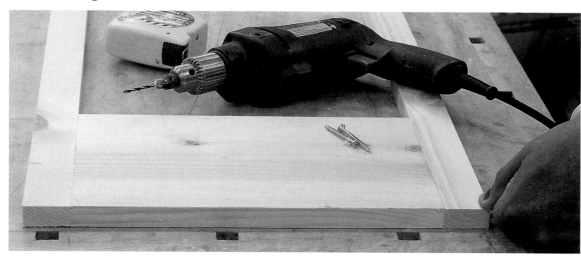

1 Build the two side frames as illustrated in the technical drawing. Join the rails A to the stiles B with glue and 2" screws through the rail edge, in counterbored holes. (Use two screws per joint.)

2 Cut a footboard D and headboard C using $^{11}\!/_{16}$" veneer particleboard or MDF. Attach the side frames to the panels using glue and 2" screws in counterbored holes. Fill the holes with wood plugs to match the type of wood you're using.

TIP *The rail-to-stile joint is an excellent application for biscuit joinery if you have a plate joiner. Dowel joinery is another alternative to screw joints. But any of the three methods will work equally well.*

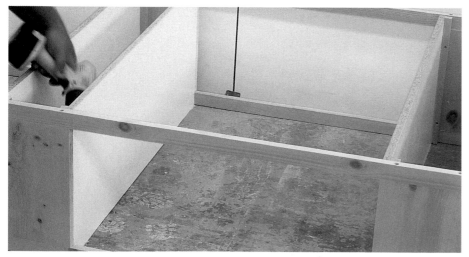

3 Prepare the four support panels E, and attach two mounting cleats F to each end of the panels. Three 1¼" screws per cleat will hold them securely. Then install the panels so they are flush with the inside edge of each drawer opening. Again, use three 1¼" screws per cleat. Insert the screws through the cleats and into the side frame assemblies.

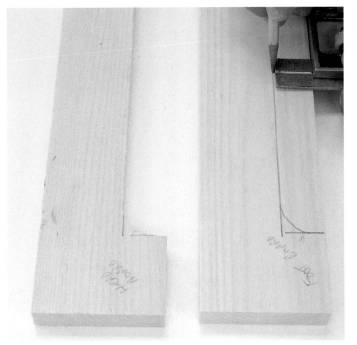

4 Cut out the shape of the footboard leg G with a jigsaw as indicated in the technical drawing, and round over the outside face but don't round the two ends, as they will join the side legs. Then cut out the side legs H and ease the edges with a ¼" roundover bit. If you don't have a router, ease the edges with sandpaper.

5 Attach the side and footboard legs using glue and 1¼" screws. Drive the screws from inside the bed frame so they won't be seen. Set the legs 1" up from the frame's bottom edge.

6 Cut out the three mattress rails J and K and ease everything except for the ends of the footboard mattress rail with a ¼" roundover bit. Attach the mattress rails to the bed frame using glue and 1¼" screws installed through the frame rail into the back of each mattress rail. Note that the mattress rails extend 2" above the top of the bed frame rails, and that the two side rails extend 6" past the head of the bed to allow for attaching the bookcase to the frame. Space the screws about 8" apart.

Building a Bookcase Headboard

1 After cutting the headboard parts to size as indicated in the materials list, attach the sides L to both the fixed shelf M and front panel N using glue and 2" screws. Counterbore all screw pilot holes and install wood plugs. Make sure the panel is flush with the side edges and attached under the fixed shelf.

2 Install the bookcase headboard top P with glue and 2" screws in counterbored holes, filled with wood plugs. Make sure to allow an overhang of 1¼" per side.

3 Attach the trim support Q with glue and small finishing nails. The support must be flush with the front edges of each side board.

4 Install the bookcase headboard trim R with glue and brad nails as shown here. The two corners require a 45° miter and the molding you choose should cover the trim support board Q. If you choose a different-size molding, modify the trim support board to match the molding height. Lastly, attach the headboard to the bed frame.

Drawer Box Construction

Drawers can be installed on one or both sides of the bed. The position of the bed in the room and the space available will dictate your setup. To illustrate one of the many options with a platform bed, I've installed a 22" and 30" drawer box. The side of my project bed will be against a wall, so I am taking advantage of the depth available with one of the drawers. Also, since the side against the wall will not be visible, I didn't close the drawer box openings. I could attach false drawer fronts or build two 16" deep drawers on both sides if the bed is accessible from that side, as well.

To make the drawers, first, cut the drawer parts from ½" Baltic birch plywood as indicated in the materials list. Follow the drawer assembly instructions as detailed in chapter two. For this bed, the drawer openings are 12"-high × 26⅞"-wide. My drawer box, using bottom-mount drawer glides, must therefore be 11"-high × 25⅞"-wide.

The drawer fronts are 12½"-high × 28"-wide. They can be made from solid glued-up wood panels, frame-and-panel fronts purchased from a cabinet door supplier in your area, or edge-taped veneer panels. I decided to use ¾" pine veneer MDF with taped edges. The iron-on edge tape is easy to apply, but it does require a little patience to trim the excess tape. However, it is a good low-cost option, and I was pleased with the results.

CONSTRUCTION OPTIONS

This project has a number of design options. Obviously, the bed can be made any width. But if you build a queen- or king-size version, add spacer boards under the support panels so the weight is distributed on the floor. This twin version has the support panels attached to each side frame only. That's fine for a narrow bed frame but extra support will be necessary on the wider models.

If you have a large room you might consider making the bookcase headboard deeper. It can be built with 1 x 12 lumber or edge taped veneer sheets of PB or MDF.

And, as we discussed earlier, drawers can be added to both sides, particularly if the bed is placed with both sides open.

If you don't need drawers but want extra storage space, the drawer fronts can be on hinges. It would be a great place to store those decorations and other items that are used for only a few days each year.

TIP *If you plan on using a mattress without a box spring you'll need a plywood base measuring ¾" x 39" x 75½". The bed rails will keep the platform properly positioned.*

CHAPTER 11

Simple Wardrobe

Many older homes have extremely small bedroom closets. This wardrobe project may be just the answer to your storage problem. This simple-to-build project is constructed with oak veneer sheet material, but it can just as easily be built from plain MDF or even particleboard. I made mine a little fancier than normal by using solid oak corner and crown molding. But again, it isn't necessary to spend the extra money if you're looking for only a plain and simple wardrobe.

Commercially made wardrobes are somewhat expensive. And if they have a drawer like the one in this project, the price really climbs. You should save a considerable sum by building your own. The final cost, however, is dependent on the type of sheet material you decide to use, the size of the wardrobe and the cost of the solid wood trim that can be added.

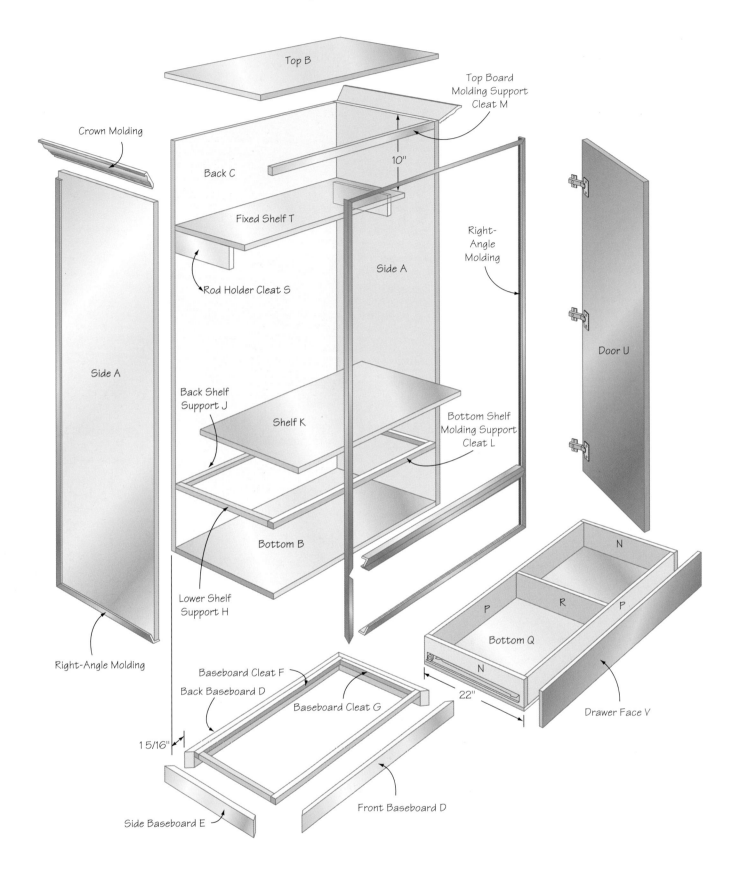

Top B

Top Board
Molding Support
Cleat M

Crown Molding

Back C

10"

Fixed Shelf T

Right-
Angle
Molding

Side A

Rod Holder Cleat S

Side A

Back Shelf
Support J

Shelf K

Bottom Shelf
Molding Support
Cleat L

N

P   R   P

Lower Shelf
Support H

Bottom B

Bottom Q

Door U

Right-Angle Molding

Baseboard Cleat F

Back Baseboard D

Baseboard Cleat G

N

22"

Drawer Face V

1 5/16"

Side Baseboard E

Front Baseboard D

Materials List • Simple Wardrobe

REF.	QTY.	PART	STOCK	THICK	WIDTH	LENGTH	COMMENTS
A	2	Sides	Veneered PB	$^{11}/_{16}$	23½	80	
B	2	Top and Bottom	Veneered PB	$^{11}/_{16}$	23½	46⅝	
C	1	Back	Veneered PB	¼	48	80	
D	2	Front/Back Baseboards	Veneered PB	$^{11}/_{16}$	3	44	
E	2	Side Baseboards	Veneered PB	$^{11}/_{16}$	3	19¾	
F	2	Baseboard Cleats	Veneered PB	¾	¾	42	
G	2	Baseboard Cleats	Veneered PB	¾	¾	17	
H	2	Lower Shelf Supports	Veneered PB	¾	¾	22¾	
J	1	Back Shelf Support	Veneered PR	¾	¾	45⅛	
K	1	Lower Shelf	Veneered PB	$^{11}/_{16}$	23½	46⅝	
L	1	Support Cleat	Hardwood	$^{11}/_{16}$	¾	46⅝	
M	1	Support Cleat	Hardwood	$^{11}/_{16}$	¾	46⅝	

Drawer Box & Shelf

REF.	QTY.	PART	STOCK	THICK	WIDTH	LENGTH	COMMENTS
N	2	Sides	Baltic Birch	½	5½	22L	
P	2	Back and Front	Baltic Birch	½	5½	44⅝	
Q	1	Bottom	Baltic Birch	½	22	46⅝	
R	1	Divider	Baltic Birch	½	5½	21	

Other Parts

REF.	QTY.	PART	STOCK	THICK	WIDTH	LENGTH	COMMENTS
S	2	Rod Holder Cleats	Hardwood	$^{11}/_{16}$	3½	14	
T	1	Shelf	Veenered PB	$^{11}/_{16}$	16	46⅝	
U	2	Doors	Veenered PB	$^{11}/_{16}$	23$^{13}/_{16}$	70	
V	1	Drawer face	Veenered PB	$^{11}/_{16}$	8½	47¾	

Hardware & Supplies

		48'-$^{11}/_{16}$" x $^{11}/_{16}$" Right-angle hardwood molding in 6'- 8' lengths
		8'-3⅛" Crown molding
	1	1½" Dia. Clothes rod
	6	107° hidden hinges
	3	handles
	1 Set	22" Bottom-mount drawer glides
		2" Wood Screws

REQUIRED TOOLS

Table or circular saw

Jigsaw or band saw

Drill

T-square jig

Combination square

Screwdrivers

Hammer

Nail set

Iron

TIP *I am using $^{11}/_{16}$" thick oak veneer particleboard for this project. The 4' by 8' sheets are heavy and awkward to handle. If you don't own a good table saw, have the lumber yard make the first cuts. They normally charge a small fee per cut but you'll avoid handling the full sheets.*

Building the Wardrobe

1 Cut the two sides A as well as the top and bottom panels B to the sizes detailed in the materials list. The panels should be flush with the ends of each side board. Attach the sides to the top and bottom boards using glue and five 2" PB screws per joint. Install the screws through the side panels and be sure to drill pilot holes for the screws to insure maximum hold.

2 Install the ¼" veneer plywood back C. Use glue and finishing nails spaced about 8" apart to hold the panel securely.

3 While the case is lying flat, build a base using parts D, E, F and G according to the dimensions in the materials list and in the technical drawing. Note that the ends are cut at 45° to form the corners. Then with glue and 1¼" PB screws, attach the base frame to the bottom of the wardrobe carcass, making sure it is mounted 2" in from all edges.

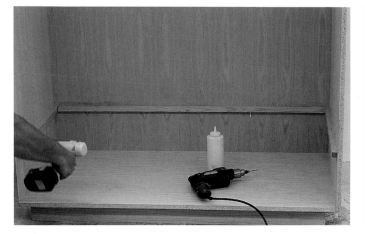

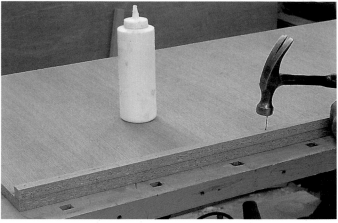

4 Cut the lower and back shelf supports H and J, and attach them to the carcase sides with 1 ¼" screws and glue from the interior of the wardrobe. The back support is held in place by using 1" screws installed through the back of the back panel and into the support. Note that the side supports are set back ¾" from the carcass side's front edges.

5 Cut the lower shelf K to size, and before installing it on the shelf support cleats, attach the molding support cleat L to the underside of the front edge using glue and brad nails. The ¹¹/₁₆" dimension of the cleat should be vertical. To verify that you have installed it correctly, the bottom shelf front thickness should be 1 ⅜".

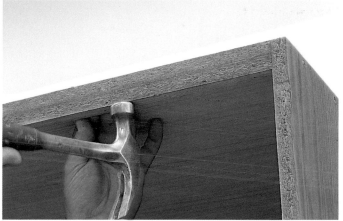

6 Apply glue to the top of all shelf supports and install the shelf. Secure it in place with a few finishing nails through the top face and into the cleats.

7 Attach support cleat M to the underside of the top board B.

TIP *Be extra careful when cutting any cabinet back. If it's cut squarely, it will "square" the cabinet you are building. You can verify that your cabinet is square by making sure the diagonal measurements are equal.*

8 Apply right-angle molding to all the edges. Carefully miter the corners at 45°angles. (See assembly drawing for details.) Apply corner molding to the front closet section as well as the drawer section. (Note that the top and shelf trim is installed on the inside of the cabinet, while the trim is on the outside at the bottom of the wardrobe). Then glue and nail the moldings to the sides and bottom edges. Stop the molding $1\frac{1}{16}$" from the top to allow room for attaching the crown.

9 With glue and finishing nails, install the crown molding at the top of the wardrobe. Note that it should be installed $\frac{11}{16}$" down from the top of each side board.

Building the Drawer Box and Attaching Hardware

This drawer box, like a few other projects in this book, is made from ½" Baltic birch plywood. For specific details on building this type of drawer, see chapter two. However, remember the rule when using bottom-mounted drawer glides: most manufacturers require ½" clearance per side. It's also good practice to leave a 1" allowance for drawer-box-to-rail clearance. For this project, I used 22" bottom-mount drawer glides and added a center divider in the box for added strength.

I After cutting the drawer box pieces to size as indicated in the materials list, assemble the pieces and sand all the edges.

2 Mount the two rod holder cleats S 10" down from the top board as shown here. Drill pilot holes and attach the cleats with glue and 1¼" screws. Plug the screw head holes with wood buttons. Apply glue on top of the rod holder cleats and secure the shelf T with a few finishing nails. This shelf should have its front edge covered with iron-on edge tape.

3 Mount a clothes rod about 12" out from the back. I've used a commercial version that is made of metal and has a good solid adhesive.

Making the Doors and Drawer Face

My doors U and drawer face V are made from $^{11}/_{16}$" veneer particleboard to which I've applied edge tape to all exposed edges before installing.

The two doors and one drawer face can be cut from one sheet of material. Before ripping the door widths, cross-cut the drawer face. Then rip the door widths. This will let the grain match on the entire front of the wardrobe.

To install the doors, use three 107° hidden hinges for each door and install following the directions in chapter one. Then secure the drawer face to the drawer box using four 1" screws through the box.

TIP *To calculate door widths when using hidden hinges, first measure the inside of the cabinet. Then, add 1" to that dimension and divide by 2. That will be the door width.*

CONSTRUCTION OPTIONS

Dozens of door options are available. Frame-and-panel models made by a door factory will be expensive, because these are large doors. The veneer particleboard doors with taped edges are reasonably priced but are very plain looking. If you want something a little fancier without spending a great deal of money, you can add some molding to the door slab.

The corner trim is an option you can eliminate. It's a different treatment and one that requires a fair amount of patience. Simply applying wood veneer edge tape to all exposed edges is an acceptable and less costly alternative.

A 1½" diameter wood dowel can be used for the hanging rod. But the metal rods are adjustable and easy to install. A wide variety of accessories is available for closets nowadays and it would be worth your time to browse through the home store for additional ideas.

As I mentioned in the introduction, less expensive sheet goods can be used if you plan on painting the wardrobe. If, for example, you need a clothing storage center in your basement, use ¾" particleboard or MDF. Give the wardrobe a couple of coats of good paint and you'll have a great storage option for all those seasonal clothes.

Metric Conversions

U.S. UNITS TO METRIC EQUIVALENTS			METRIC UNITS TO U.S. EQUIVALENTS		
To convert from	Multiply by	To get	To convert from	Multiply by	To get
Inches	25.4	Millimeters	Millimeters	0.0394	Inches
Inches	2.54	Centimeters	Centimeters	0.3937	Inches
Feet	30.48	Centimeters	Centimeters	0.0328	Feet
Feet	0.3048	Meters	Meters	3.2808	Feet
Yards	0.9144	Meters	Meters	1.0936	Yards
Square inches	6.4516	Square centimeters	Square centimeters	0.1550	Square inches
Square feet	0.0929	Square meters	Square meters	10.764	Square feet
yards	0.8361	Square meters	Square meters	1.1960	Square yards
Acres	0.4047	Hectares	Hectares	2.4711	Acres
Cubic inches	16.387	Cubic centimeters	Cubic centimeters	0.0610	Cubic inches
Cubic feet	0.0283	Cubic meters	Cubic meters	35.315	Cubic feet
Cubic feet	28.316	Liters	Liters	0.0353	Cubic feet
Cubic yards	0.7646	Cubic meters	Cubic meters	1.308	Cubic yards
Cubic yards	764.55	Liters	Liters	0.0013	Cubic yards
Ounces (fluid)	0.0296	Liters	Liters	33.784	Ounces (fluid)
Pints	0.4732	Liters	Liters	2.1133	Pints
Quarts	0.9464	Liters	Liters	1.0566	Quarts
Gallons	3.7854	Liters	Liters	0.2642	Gallons
Ounces (weight)	28.350	Grams	Grams	0.3527	Ounces (weight)
Pounds	0.4536	Kilograms	Kilograms	2.2046	Pounds

Lumber

WOOD SIZE (MILLIMETERS)	NEAREST U.S. EQUIVALENT (INCHES)
25× 75	1× 3
50× 100	2×4
50× 150	2×6
50× 200	2×8
50× 250	2×10
50× 300	2×12

Fractions to Metric Equivalents

INCHES	MILLIMETERS	INCHES	MILLIMETERS	INCHES	MILLIMETERS	INCHES	MILLIMETERS
1/64	0.396875	17/64	6.746875	33/64	13.096880	49/64	19.446880
1/32	0.793750	9/32	7.143750	17/32	13.493750	25/32	19.843750
3/64	1.190625	19/64	7.540625	35/64	13.890630	51/64	20.240630
1/16	1.587500	5/16	7.937500	9/16	14.287500	13/16	20.637500
5/64	1.984375	21/64	8.334375	37/64	14.684380	53/64	21.034380
3/32	2.381250	11/32	8.731250	19/32	15.081250	27/32	21.431250
7/64	2.778125	23/64	9.128125	39/64	15.478130	55/64	21.828130
1/8	3.175000	3/8	9.525000	5/8	15.875000	7/8	22.225000
9/64	3.571875	25/64	9.921875	41/64	16.271880	57/64	22.621880
5/32	3.968750	13/32	10.318750	21/32	16.668750	29/32	23.018750
11/64	4.365625	27/64	10.715630	43/64	17.065630	59/64	23.415630
3/16	4.762500	7/16	11.112500	11/16	17.462500	15/16	23.812500
13/64	5.159375	29/64	11.509380	45/64	17.859380	61/64	24.209380
7/32	5.556250	15/32	11.906250	23/32	18.256250	31/32	24.606250
15/64	5.953125	31/64	12.303130	47/64	18.653130	63/64	25.003130
1/4	6.350000	1/2	12.700000	3/4	19.050000	1	25.400000

CHAPTER 12

Home Entertainment Center

This is the most challenging project in the book. But analyze the modules, break down the larger sections into small components, and I believe you will see that it isn't all that complicated.

This entertainment center was built to suit my needs. There are large cubes for speakers, a wide tower for a 32" television, a pullout for a record turntable, and many CD and tape storage drawers. Your needs may be different, so alter the partitions accordingly.

The pullout has full-extension drawer glides. The large television is mounted on a lazy-susan style mechanism that's available in most hardware stores. The component areas are fitted with smoked glass doors to allow most remote controls to operate with the doors closed.

I decided to use ¾" oak plywood veneer board. It's strong and can withstand greater loads than particleboard over wide shelf spans. Plywood core veneer board is more expensive than particle core, but I believe it's warranted in this case.

I also considered how to hide the large television and decided pocket doors were the best option. I'll detail how these sliders are mounted.

I purchased factory-made wood doors and had 5mm gray glass with polished edges fabricated for my glass doors.

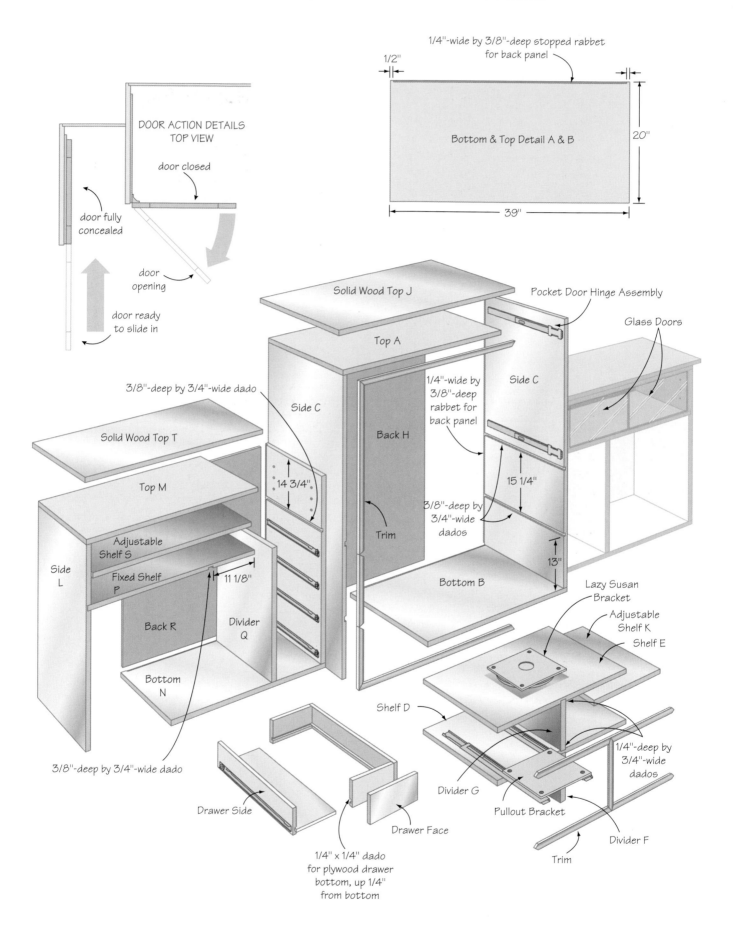

1/4"-wide by 3/8"-deep stopped rabbet for back panel

1/2"

Bottom & Top Detail A & B

20"

39"

DOOR ACTION DETAILS
TOP VIEW

door closed

door fully concealed

door opening

door ready to slide in

Solid Wood Top J

Pocket Door Hinge Assembly

Top A

Glass Doors

3/8"-deep by 3/4"-wide dado

Side C

Side C

Back H

1/4"-wide by 3/8"-deep rabbet for back panel

Solid Wood Top T

14 3/4"

15 1/4"

Top M

3/8"-deep by 3/4"-wide dados

Adjustable Shelf S

Trim

Side L

Fixed Shelf P

11 1/8"

Bottom B

13"

Back R

Divider Q

Lazy Susan Bracket

Adjustable Shelf K

Shelf E

Bottom N

Shelf D

1/4"-deep by 3/4"-wide dados

3/8"-deep by 3/4"-wide dado

Divider G

Pullout Bracket

Divider F

Drawer Side

Drawer Face

Trim

1/4" x 1/4" dado for plywood drawer bottom, up 1/4" from bottom

Building the Center Tower

Materials List • Center Tower

REF.	QTY.	PART	STOCK	THICK	WIDTH	LENGTH	COMMENTS
A	1	Top	Veneered Ply	¾	28	38	
B	1	Bottom	Veneered Ply	¾	28	38	
C	2	Sides	Veneered Ply	¾	28	65½	
D	1	Fixed Shelf	Veneered Ply	¾	27¾	37¼	
E	1	Fixed Shelf	Veneered Ply	¾	27¾	37¼	
F	1	Divider	Veneered Ply	¾	13¼	27¾	
G	1	Divider	Veneered Ply	¾	15¾	27¾	
H	1	Back	Veneered Ply	¼	37⅛	66⅛	
J	1	Solid Wood top	Oak	¾	29	40	
K	1	Adjustable Shelf	Veneered Ply	¾	18⅛	27	
	1	Base	Veneered Ply	¾	26	34	
	1	TV Turntable Platform	Veneered Ply	¾	18½	28½	
	1	Pullout Platform	Veneered Ply	¾	16⅞	18	

Hardware & Supplies

1	1" x 12" Oak side trim
2	1" x 12" Oak side trim
	26'-¾"-Wide Trim
2	18¼" x 35½" TV Pocket Doors
2	17¾" x 13" Album Storage Doors
2	14¹³⁄₁₆" x 17¾" Glass Doors
	1" and 2" Wood Screws
	Brad Nails
	Carpenter's Glue
	Preglued Iron-on Edge Tape
	Decorative Bolts
	Plastic Wire Grommets
	⅜" Wood Plugs
2 sets	20" Pocket Door Hardware
	Hidden Hinges
6	Door Knobs
2 sets	Lazy-Susan Pullout Hardware
4	Door Catches

REQUIRED TOOLS

Table or circular saw

Drill

Router

T-square jig

Combination square

Screwdrivers

Hammer

Nail set

1 Cut the top and bottom A and B. Each board will require a ¼"-wide by ⅜"-deep stopped dado to receive the backpanel. Stop the dado ½" from each end. The top of the bottom board B and the bottom A of the top board must each be dadoed. Then apply preglued iron-on edge tape to both ends of boards A and B.

2 Cut the two tower sides C. Both sides require dadoes and a back rabbet on each inside face. All of the cuts are ⅜" deep. Refer to the diagram for rabbet and dado positions.

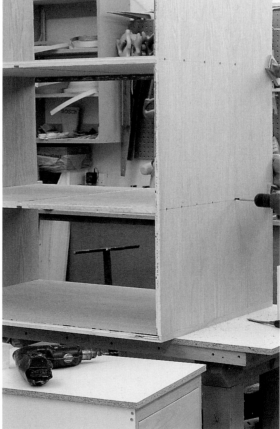

3 Prepare shelf D by cutting dadoes ¼"-deep by ¾"-wide, in the center on it's top and bottom. Handle this board carefully, as it will be weak at the cut until it's installed. Shelf E is cut like shelf D; however only one dado is needed in the center on the bottom face. Then attach the top A and bottom B to the tower sides C making certain all dadoes and rabbets are properly aligned. Use glue and 2" wood screws. Predrill the screw holes.

4 Install shelves D and E in their respective dadoes. Use carpenter's glue and screw through the outside of the cabinet sides into the shelves using 2" wood screws. Start your screws 10" back from the front edges so the screws will be hidden by the side towers.

5 Cut and install dividers F and G. Apply glue and clamp in place until they set.

6 Next, install the ¼" back in the rabbets. Apply a fine bead of glue and secure the board with brad nails. This board must be cut square, as it will help to correctly align the cabinet.

7 We need a strong base to support the large television, equipment and record albums that will be stored in the unit. I want to slightly elevate the unit but still maintain as much contact with the floor as possible. To achieve this, install a ¾" base to the underside of bottom B. Attach the base 2" in from the sides and front with glue and 1¼" wood screws.

8 Trim the outside front and sides edges of the base with ¾"-thick by 1"-wide solid wood. Attach these strips to the cabinet base with glue and 1¼" wood screws. The side pieces need to only be 12" long because the side towers cover a portion of the center tower.

Building the Side Towers

Two side towers are required. They are mirror images of each other in my project. If you plan to build the same setup, mark the right and left pieces to avoid mistakes.

Materials List • Side Towers

REF.	QTY.	PART	STOCK	THICK	WIDTH	LENGTH	COMMENTS
L	4	Sides	Veneered Ply	¾	20	44½	
M	2	Tops	Veneered Ply	¾	20	39	
N	2	Bottoms	Veneered Ply	¾	20	39	
P	2	Fixed Shelves	Veneered Ply	¾	19¾	38¼	
Q	2	Dividers	Veneered Ply	¾	19¾	29⅜	
R	2	Backs	Veneered Ply	¼	38¾	45⅛	
S	2	Adjustable Shelves	Veneered Ply	¾	19	37⅜	
T	2	Solid Wood Tops	Oak	¾	21	40	
	2	Bases	Veneered Ply	¾	18	38	

Hardware & Supplies

2	1" x 39" Front trim	
2	1" x 18" Side trim	
	56'-¾"-Wide Trim	
2	10⅝" x 28⅞" Wood doors	
4	14¹⁵⁄₁₆" x 18⅝" Glass doors	
	2" Wood Screws	
2	Door Knobs	
4	Hidden Hinges	
	Shelf Pins	

Cut the four sides L and rout the dadoes and rabbets on the inside face of each panel. You will need two right and two left side panels. The tops M and bottoms N are the same size. Cut the ¼"-wide by ⅜"-deep stopped dado on the underside of the top boards M and top side of the bottom boards N as shown. Mark the panels, noting their final position, and apply oak tape to the edge that will be visible.

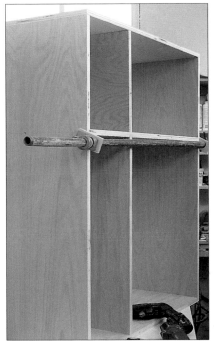

TIP *Cut a board 1⁄16" higher than the upper cavity dimension and carefully wedge it in place over the vertical divider dado joint. The pressure will tighten the joint until it sets.*

2 Cut the two fixed shelves P and rout the dado as shown in the technical drawing. Secure the tops M and bottoms N to the side panels. Use glue and 2" wood screws in piloted holes from the top and bottom of each board. Verify that the finished edges are oriented properly on each tower.

3 Install the middle fixed shelves P in the dadoes. Remember, there is a right and left position for each shelf in the towers. Apply glue to the joint and clamp until dry. The shelves are set flush with the front edges of the side panels.

4 Cut the vertical divider panels Q and glue them into the dado. The bottom ends of each panel are glued and 2" wood screws are installed from the underside of the bottom board to secure the dividers. Make certain the divider is parallel to the side panel. The panel must be accurately positioned to permit proper fitting of the inset doors.

Next install the 1⁄4" back panel R using glue and brad nails. Attach the 3⁄4" plywood base to the side towers in the same way the center tower base was installed. However, it's positioned 2" in from the one side and front edges of the cabinets. The base should extend 1" past the side that attaches to the center tower. The extended base will meet the center tower base. (Remember to install right and left bases.) Then install the base trim as shown here.

Connecting the Towers

2 Build a shelf pin-hole jig from scrap lumber. I've used 1" on-center spacing. A short length of dowel rod on my drill bit guarantees the correct hole depth.

1 Secure the sides L to the center tower using decorative bolts. Many styles are available, so choose one that matches the cabinet hardware.

3 Plastic wire grommets are available at most hardware stores. Install them in shelves and partitions so all the equipment can be connected.

Building and Installing the Solid Wood Tops

1 The solid wood tops can be purchased at many home stores in standard sizes. If you have the clamps available, tops can be made by edge-gluing a number of boards together. If you don't have the equipment to dress the edges, many lumberyards will provide that service for a small fee.

2 Cut the tops J and T to size according to the materials lists and sand all the surfaces smooth. Then install each top with six 1" wood screws in pre-drilled holes from inside the cabinet. Counterbore the holes before installing the screws so they can be filled with wood plugs.

Installing the Edge Trim

The trim I've used is available in most lumber stores. It's ¾" wide with a molded pattern on the face.

1 Attach the trim with glue and an electric brad nailer if you have one. If not, use ¾" brads and set the nails. Use a 45°miter at all right-angled corners.

2 When a shelf intersects a vertical panel, a special cut is required. The molding meeting a run at 90°is cut at a 45° angle when it's in the standing position on your miter box. The back cut allows the intersecting run to fit tightly. The cut may require a little sanding, and the angle is dependent on the style of molding used. It's a little fussy at times and requires a few trial cuts to get a good fit.

Installing the Glass Doors

Before ordering or making doors, build the cabinet. Inset doors must be correctly sized for a proper fit. The door spacing depends a great deal on the type of hinge hardware. To get a perfect fit, purchase the hardware and make a sample door with scrap lumber.

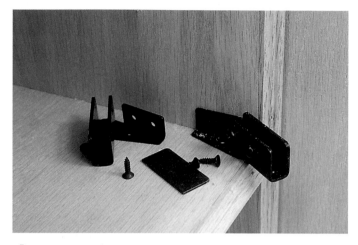

1 Install the glass-door hinges. I've used an inset-style hinge that doesn't require holes drilled in the glass.

2 The door handles I've used slip onto the glass and are held in place with a foam gasket.

Fitting the Wood Inset Doors

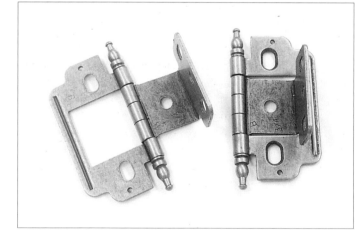

1 The hardware I've used for this project is a traditional North American-style inset hinge.

2 Install the hinges 2" from the bottom and top edges of the door. Shim the door in its proper open position and secure the door to the cabinet. Most hinges will provide a little adjustment so install screws in the center of the adjustment slot. Test the door operation and adjust if necessary. Install the remaining doors using the same procedure.

Attaching the Pocket Doors

I've used pocket door hardware by Blum for this project. Follow the manufacturer's installation procedures that are included with your hardware.

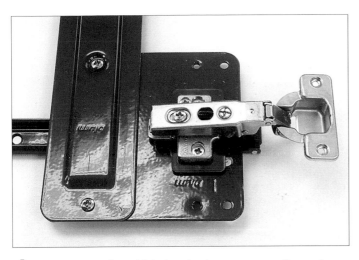

| Assemble the right and left door hardware sets according to the instructions.

2 My doors are ¾" thick, so I have set the door stops 1" back from the front edge of the cabinet. That distance includes ¾" for the door thickness and ¼" for the hinge hardware. Attach the top rail with one screw in the front hole. Measure the same set-back for the bottom rail bumper and install a screw in the front of that rail. Level the top rail and secure the back with a screw. Before securing the bottom rail, check the roller operation making sure the mechanism hits the bottom and top bumper at the same time. If it's operating correctly, install the track screws.

TIP *You can accurately locate the hinge positions on the door by first attaching the hinge body to the door hardware. Next, locate and mark the center of the hinge with a marker pen on the hinge flange. Hold or shim the door in its correct open position and transfer that mark to the door. Both hinges should be marked on the door. The Blum hinges supplied with the pocket-door set recommend that the 35mm hole in the door be set back ³⁄₁₆" from the edge of the door. Drill the holes and install both hinges.*

3 Attach the door and test for proper operation. The hidden hinges allow the doors to be adjusted in three directions. Quite often, adjustment and trial fitting is necessary when installing pocket doors.

Attaching a Television Lazy Susan

1 The size and style of a lazy-susan platform depends on the hardware you purchase. Each manufacturer has a different method, so read the installation instructions with your hardware.

2 My television platform for the lazy-susan hardware is a ¾"-thick piece of veneer plywood. You can apply edge tape or attach ½"-thick solid wood strips to all four edges as I've done.

TIP *If you use the solid wood edging for your television platform, round over the top edges. The wood strips can be attached with glue and finishing nails. Set the nails and fill the holes with a colored putty stick that matches your final finish.*

Making a Turntable Pull-Out

1 Whenever you install pullouts behind cabinet doors, attach a ¾" wood spacer. That spacer allows the pullout enough clearance to move past the door hinges. This spacer or cleat is required only on the hinge side. Remember to reduce the cabinet width by ¾" when calculating the pullout width.

2 Build the pullout platform using ¾"-thick veneer plywood with taped edges. The front on my platform has decorative molding applied, which can be used as a handle.

3 Install two strips of ¾" x 1½" wood on the bottom of the pullout. The spacing depends on which style of drawer glides you are using. Mine require ½" on each side. Therefore, the support distance equals the cabinet interior width, minus the wood spacer and the ½" clearance per side for the drawer glides.

4 I've installed full-extension, side-mounted drawer glides. Be sure to set the pullout back far enough into the cabinet so the inset glass door can close properly.

Building Storage Pullouts

Pullout drawers are a great addition to any entertainment center. They help organize all the CDs, audio cassettes, videocassettes and associated hardware.

These drawers are simple boxes made of cabinet-grade ½"-thick plywood. I have attached a drawer face to the box that matches the cabinet material.

Materials List • Storage Pullouts

REF.	QTY.	PART	STOCK	THICK	WIDTH	LENGTH	COMMENTS
	8	Cleats	Hardwood	¾	1½	18¾	
	16	Sides	Baltic Birch	½	3	18	
	8	Fronts	Baltic Birch	½	3	8	
	8	Backs	Baltic Birch	½	2½	8	
	8	Bottoms	Baltic Birch	¼	8½	17¾	
	8	Drawer Faces	Veneered Ply	¾	9⅞	3½	

Hardware & Supplies

8 Sets	18" Full-extension side-mounted drawer glides
	1" and 1¼" Wood Screws
	Finishing Nails
	Carpenter's Glue

FACTORS DETERMINING DRAWER WIDTH

Most drawer glides require ½" clearance on both sides to operate. That means the drawer box exterior dimensions must be 1" less than the opening. Because we have to use wood cleats for the door clearance, we must also subtract the width of the cleat when calculating drawer sizes. My drawer box width equals a side to side cabinet measurement of 10¾", minus the thickness of the ¾" cleat, less the ½" per side spacing for drawer hardware. In this example, the drawer box is 9" wide.

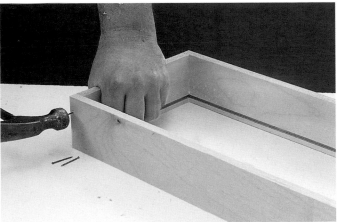

1 Attach the 8 cleats to the cabinet on the door-hinge side. Use three 1¼" wood screws per cleat and space them 6" apart starting from the bottom board. Then cut all the sides, fronts and backs as detailed in the materials list from ½" Baltic birch plywood. Make a ¼"-wide by ¼"-deep groove ¼" above the bottom edge of each side and front board.

2 For each pullout, attach the side boards to the front with glue and finishing nails. Check that the grooves for the bottom are aligned before nailing.

3 Install the back with glue and nails. It is ½" lower and its top edge is aligned with the side board top edges.

4 Slide the bottom into the grooves. It should be flush with the back face of the back when correctly positioned. Use finishing nails to secure it to the back panel.

5 Cut and install the drawer front. Use 1" screws from the inside to secure the front to the box.

Completing the Cabinet

Remove all the hardware, fill any nail holes, and give the cabinet a final sanding before finishing. To finish the piece, I used a 50 percent mixture of Minwax Provincial and Puritan Pine stains. After staining, I applied three coats of polyurethane.

After the finish is dry, install the hardware. Drawer glides should be installed according to the manufacturer's instructions. All the pullout hardware in my unit are 18" full-extension side-mounted glides. They provide full access to the drawers where my CDs and cassettes will be stored.

Wood Color Guide

COLOR	WOOD	COST	NOTES
White	Aspen	$	
	Silver maple	$$	
	Spruce (Adirondack spruce, blue spruce, skunk spruce)	$	
	Eastern white pine	$	Pines have high pitch content that can ruin blades; use blade lubricant
	Sugar pine	$$	See above
	Western white pine	$	See above
	Holly	$$$	Discolors if the wood is not cut properly
	Basswood (American lime)	$	Turns pale brown on exposure
	Hard maple (rock maple, sugar maple)	$$	
	European ash (English/French/etc. ash)	$$	Turns light brown on exposure
Black	Black walnut	$$	
	Wenge	$$$	
	South American walnut	$$$	
	Ebony (gaboon)	$$$	Difficult to machine; endangered
Red	Bloodwood (Brazil redwood, cardinal wood, pau rainha)	$$$	Cuts poorly; use no.9 Precision Ground blade on band saw
	Aromatic cedar (eastern red cedar, chest cedar, Tennessee cedar)	$	Often has internal stress cracks; when cutting into small pieces, wood may break
	Cherry	$$	
	Jarrah	$$	Moderately difficult to work
	Brazilwood (pernambuco wood, Bahia wood, para wood)	$$$	Endangered
	African padauk (camwood, barwood)	$$	Endangered
	Red heart	$$$	
Yellow	Pau amarillo	$$	Brightest; canary yellow
	Oosage orange	$$	Turns orange-brown on exposure
	Yellow cedar (Alaska cedar, Nootka cypress, yellow cypress)	$$	
	Yellow pine	$	
	Ponderosa pine (western yellow pine, Californian white pine)	$	Knots can cause problems when planing
	Caragana	$	Actually a shrub; have to look for it
	Hickory	$$	
	Yellowheart	$$	
	Satinwood (East Indian satinwood)	$$$	Moderately difficult to work
	Obeche (ayous, wawa, arere)	$	Keep cutting edges sharp; endangered
Green	Staghorn sumac (velvet sumac)	$	Grows as shrub orsmall tree; not commercially available; grows in northeast U.S. and eastern Canada
	American yellow poplar (tulip tree, canary wood, canoewood)	$	Must search out green or gray heartwood
	Verawood (maracaibo, lignum vitae, guayacan)	$$$	Hard to cut; hard to get finish to stick because wood is oily or waxy; polyurathane finish will highlight color; finish pieces before gluing project
Blue/Gray	Spruce (Adirondack spruce, blue spruce, skunk spruce)	$	Some spruce boards have gray or blue cast; rare
	Blue mahoe (mahoe, mountain mahoe, seaside mahoe)	$$$	Heartwood varies from purple, metallic blue, olive brown; must search for blue; rare
Purple	Purpleheart (violetwood, pau roxo)	$$	Burns easily; use precision-ground blade on scroll saw or bandsaw; be careful not to burn wood while sanding
Orange	Osage orange	$$	Cuts yellow, then turns orange on exposure
	African padauk (comwood, barwood, corail)	$$	Heartwood can be found in bright orange hue
	Zebrawood	$$$	Dark streaks through wood
	Red gum (sweet gum, alligator wood, hazel pine)	$$	Streaks of red and black; beautiful grain

Legend: $ Free or inexpensive

$$ Moderately priced

$$$ Expensive

Common Woodworking Terms

BEVEL A cut that is not 90° to a board's face; or the facet left by such a cut.

BISCUIT A thin, flat oval of compressed beech that is inserted between two pieces of wood into mating saw kerfs made by a biscuit-or plate-joining machine.

BRIDLE JOINT A joint that combines features of both lap joints and mortise and tenon. It has a U-shaped mortise in the end of the board.

BUTT JOINT Two flat faces of mating parts that fit flush together with no interlocking joinery.

CARPENTER'S GLUE White and yellow adhesives formulated for use with wood.

CASING The trim framing a window, door or other opening.

CHALK LINE Line made by snapping a chalk-coated string against a plane.

CHECK A crack in wood material caused by drying, either just in the surface or in the ends of the board so the fibers have separated.

COMPOUND MITER A cut where the blade path is not perpendicular to the wood's end or edge and the blade tilt is not 90° to the face.

COPING Sawing a negative profile in one piece to fit the positive profile of another, usually in molding.

COUNTERBORE A straight-sided drilled hole that recesses a screw head below the wood surface so a wood plug can cover it, or the bit that makes this hole.

COUNTERSINK A cone-shaped drilled hole whose slope angle matches the underside of a flat screw head and sinks it flush with the wood surface, or the tool that makes this hole.

CROSSCUT To saw wood perpendicular to the grain.

CUPPING A drying defect where one side of the board shrinks more across the grain than the other, causing the board to curl in on itself like a trough.

DADO A flat-bottomed, U-shaped milling cut of varying widths and depths but always running across the grain.

DOVETAIL JOINT A traditional joint characterized by interlocking fingers and pockets shaped like its name. It has exceptional resistance to tension.

DOWEL A small cylinder of wood that is used to reinforce a wood joint.

DRESSING The process of turning rough lumber into a smooth board with flat, parallel faces and straight, parallel edges and whose edges are square to the face.

EDGE LAP A notch into the edge of a board halfway across its width that forms half of an edge lap joint.

FINGERLAP A specific joint of the lap family that has straight, interwoven fingers; also called a box joint.

FINISH Varnish, stain, paint or any mixture that protects a surface.

FLAT-SAWN The most common cut of lumber where the growth rings run predominantly across the end of the board; or its characteristic grain pattern.

FLUSH Level with an adjoining surface.

GRAIN PATTERN The visual appearance of wood grain. Types of grain pattern include flat, straight, curly, quilted, rowed, mottled, crotch, cathedral, bees wing or bird's-eye.

HARDWOOD Wood from broadleaf deciduous trees, no matter what the density. (Balsa is a hardwood.)

HEARTWOOD Wood from the core of a tree, usually darker and harder than newer wood.

JIG A shop-made or aftermarket device that assists in positioning and steadying the wood or tools.

JOINTING The process of making a board face straight and flat or an edge straight, whether by hand or machine.

KERF The visible path of subtracted wood left by a saw blade.

KEY An inserted joint-locking device, usually made of wood.

KNOCKDOWN JOINT A joint that is assembled without glue and can be disassembled and reassembled if necessary.

LAP JOINT A type of joint made by removing half the thickness or width of the parts and lapping them over each other.

LENGTH JOINT A joint that makes one longer wood unit out of two shorter ones by joining them end to end.

LEVEL Absolutely horizontal.

MILLING The process of removing material to leave a desired positive or negative profile in the wood.

MITER A generic term meaning mainly an angled cut across the face grain, or specifically 45° cut across the face or end grain or along the grain. See also *bevel*.

MORTISE The commonly rectangular or round pocket into which a mating tenon is inserted. Mortises can be blind (stop inside the wood thickness), through, or open on one end.

PARTICLEBOARD A panel made of wood particles and glue.

PILOT HOLE A small, drilled hole used as a guide and pressure relief for screw insertion, or to locate additional drilling work like countersinking and counterboring.

PLYWOOD Panel made by laminating layers of wood.

QUARTERSAWN A stable lumber cut where the growth rings on the board's end run more vertically across the end than horizontally and the grain on the face looks straight; also called straight-grained or rift-sawn.

RABBET A milled cut that leaves a flat step parallel to, but recessed from, the wood's surface.

RAIL The horizontal parts of a door frame.

RIP To cut parallel to the grain of a board.

SAPWOOD The new wood in a tree, located between the core (heartwood) and bark; usually lighter in color.

SCARF JOINT A joint that increases the overall length of wood by joining two pieces at their ends, commonly by gluing together two unusually long bevels in their faces or edges.

SCRIBE To make layout lines or index marks using a knife or awl.

SHOULDER The perpendicular face of a step cut like a rabbet that bears against a mating joint part to stabilize the joint.

SOFTWOOD Wood from coniferous evergreen trees, no matter what the density. (Yew is a softwood.)

SPLINE A flat, thin strip of wood that fits into mating grooves between two parts to reinforce the joint between them.

STAIN A pigment or dye used to color wood through saturation; or a discoloration in wood from fungus or chemicals.

STILE The vertical parts of a door frame.

TENON The male part of a mortise and tenon joint, commonly rectangular or round, but not restricted to those shapes.

TONGUE AND GROOVE Joinery method in which one board is cut with a protruding groove and another is cut with a matching groove along its edge.

TWISTING A drying defect in lumber that causes it to twist so the faces at the end of the board are in a different plane.

VENEER A thin sheet of wood bonded to another material.

WIDTH JOINT A joint that makes a unit of the parts by joining them edge to edge to increase the overall width of wood.

Common Wood Defects

KNOT A dark whorl from a cross section of a branch. Knots weaken wood and affect appearance.

BARK POCKETS An encased area of bark in a board. Bark pockets reduce strength and lessen appearance.

INSECT DAMAGE Insects can cause holes that reduce board strength.

FUNGAL DAMAGE Fungi can stain wood. Called spalting, wood with advanced fungal decay may be weakened and, when cut, will release spores that can cause severe allergic reactions.

CHECK A separation between growth rings at the end of a board. Checks are common and lessen appearance, but do not weaken wood unless deep.

SHAKE A separation between growth rings that results in a slat coming loose from the face of the board.

GUM A sticky accumulation of resin that bleeds through finishes.

PITCH POCKETS Pitch-filled spaces between grain layers. Pitch pockets may bleed after a board is milled and occasionally bleed through finishes.

MACHINE BURN Blunt planer knives may burn the face of the board.

MACHINE WAVES Incorrect planer speeds may create waves on the face of the wood. Boards with waves must be thinned again.

BOW An end-to-end warp along the face of the board. Bowed boards are fit for horizontal load-bearing if placed convex side up.

CUP An edge-to-edge warp across the face of the board. Cupped boards are fit for non-load-bearing use if placed convex side up or out.

CROOK An end-to-end warp along the board edge. Crooked boards are fit for horizontal load-bearing if placed convex side up.

TWIST A lopsided or uneven warp. Wood is weakened, but twisted boards are fit for non-load-bearing use.

Index